ILLINOIS:

Its People and Culture

ILLINOIS:

Its People and Culture

By
ANN LATHROP
WALTER B. HENDRICKSON JR.
W. E. ROSENFELT

Publishers

T. S. DENISON & COMPANY, INC.

Minneapolis

 T. S. DENISON & COMPANY, INC.

Standard Book Number: 513-01381-4
Printed in the United States of America
by The Brings Press

Copyright © MCMLXXV by T. S. Denison & Co., Inc.
Minneapolis, Minn. 55437

Foreword

Furs, farms and factories have all been important in the wondrous story of Illinois. Perhaps the most important part of the story of Illinois is the faith of her people, faith that they could take the materials with which nature had blessed the land and build a good life for themselves and their neighbors.

The Indians were the first to see and appreciate the beauty and bounty of Illinois. They fished in the gently flowing rivers and hunted for food in the forests. They helped Illinoisans to appreciate the beauty and natural bounty of the land.

The French built a fur empire in Illinois. They trapped along the rivers and streams, and they introduced the European culture to the Illinois country.

The Yankees and Southerners came and settled on farms where they used the rich prairie soil to produce the agricultural products for which Illinois became famous.

Later, people came from Europe and other parts of the world to work in the factories and mines that use the materials from beneath the soil of Illinois.

Today, the people of the state realize that they must work to preserve and conserve the beauty and resources of the Prairie State to continue the heritage of those who came before them.

In order to understand the history of the world we live in, we must begin by understanding the history of the things that are familiar to us. By studying the history of our state, we will begin the lifelong adventure of the study of history.

The wondrous story of our state as presented in this book, "Illinois: Its People and Culture," will give us an excellent start on that adventure.

—Neil W. Lathrop,
President, Illinois Historical Society
Chairman, Department of Social Science,
Highland Community College

DEDICATION

To the students in the schools of Illinois today, who will be the leaders of tomorrow. May you find true meaning in your cultural heritage as so beautifully stated in the following words of wisdom by one of Illinois' most beloved sons.

> When a nation goes down and never comes back, when a society or civilization perishes, one condition may always be found. They lose sight of what brought them along.
>
> —Carl Sandburg

ACKNOWLEDGMENTS

Amtrak Intercity Railroad Passenger Service / Kee T. Chang, Photos / Chicago Historical Society / Chicago Association of Commerce and Industry / Chicago Convention and Tourism Bureau / Chicago Museum of Science and Industry / Chicago Tribune, Sports Department / Commonwealth Edison / Deere and Company / Ford Motor Company, Education Affairs Department / Griggsville Wild Bird Society / Governor's Office For Human Resources / Handbook of Illinois Government / Hedrich-Blessing / Illinois State Historical Library / Illinois State Museum / Illinois Department of Conservation / Illinois Archaeological Survey / Illinois Division of Tourism / Illinois State Historical Society / Illinois Department of Transportation / Illinois Industrial Location Guide / Illinois Information Service / Illinois Department of Business and Economic Development / Illinois Central Gulf Railroad / Library of Congress / L. LaFrance, Brookfield Zoo / National Aeronautics and Space Administration / National Air Museum, Smithsonian Institute / Norman Templin Photos / Nebraska Historical Society / Ozark Airlines / Office of Thomas C. Rose, State Representative, 49th District / Pioneer Seed Corn Company / R. Patrick White / Sears, Roebuck and Company / University of Illinois Library / University of Illinois / WJIL Radio, Jacksonville.

SPECIAL ACKNOWLEDGMENT

Olive S. Foster, Supervisor of School Services, Illinois State Historical Library
Orvetta Robinson, Librarian, Illinois State Museum
Milton D. Thompson, Director, Illinois State Museum
Neil W. Lathrop, President, 1974, Illinois Historical Society

SPECIAL MAPS AND ILLUSTRATIONS BY HOWARD LINDBERG

Cover Photo, The Webb Company

Contents

Introduction

This is the story of Illinois! Discover the land, the people and the events that have made this state such a wonderful place to live. Illinois is often referred to as "The Prairie State," because of the many acres of rich, rolling farmland. Some prefer to think of Illinois as the home of the "Illini" or "Illiniwek," the name by which the early Indians referred to themselves. (Illiniwek meant "the men" in their language.) This land was the home of several Indian tribes long before the first white men came to the area. The many lakes and rivers provided a means of transportation for these people, as well as providing food and furs from the many fish and animals living in or near the water.

The official state slogan refers to our state as "The Land of Lincoln," in honor of Abraham Lincoln, perhaps the most famous of all the people who have called the state their home.

In this book we will try to learn what the land and its people have contributed to our present-day Illinois. We will look at these peoples' customs, their problems and actions, and attempt to find out where we fit into this overall picture of present-day Illinois. Our state is waiting for you to discover its many interesting secrets!

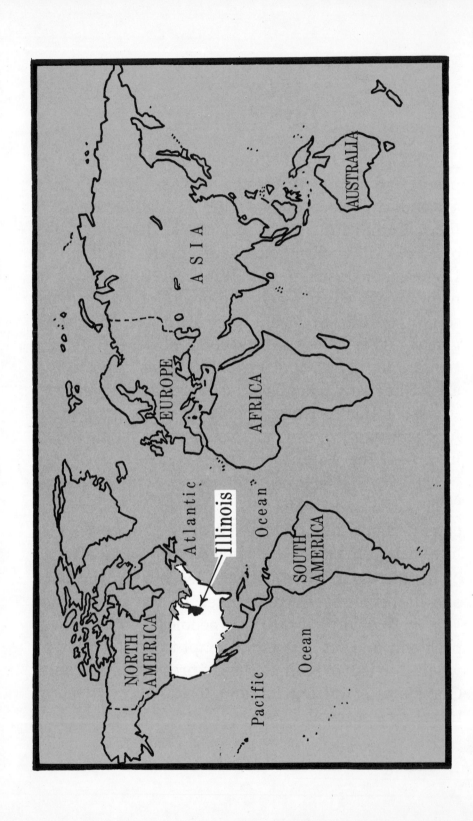

Chapter I

The Geography of Illinois

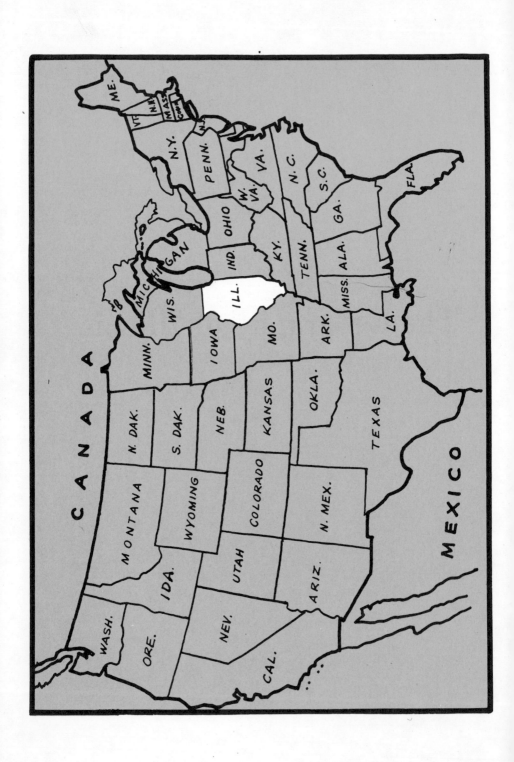

Location

Illinois may seem quite large to you, but it is really only a small part of the world we live in. It is one of the fifty states that make up the United States, and only a small area on the **continent** of North America. The continent of North America is but one of several continents that make up our **global** world, so you see, the portion of the globe we call Illinois is really very small indeed. If all the land area of the world would suddenly disappear, leaving only Illinois, it would appear as a tiny speck in a vast ocean.

Land Area

We have described Illinois as a small part of the global land area, although it is very large in some ways. Suppose you were to walk from east to west across the state, from one border to the other. Do you know how long it would take you? (The distance is approximately 218 miles.) For those who would like to walk across the state from north to south, the distance is approximately 385 miles. How long would this take?

Terrain

Elevation refers to the distance the land rises above **sea level.** Mountainous states such as Colorado and Wyoming have some points of land rising as high as 14,000 feet above sea level. Illinois is not a mountainous state, and the highest point in the state rises to 1,241 feet above sea level. This is called Charles

15

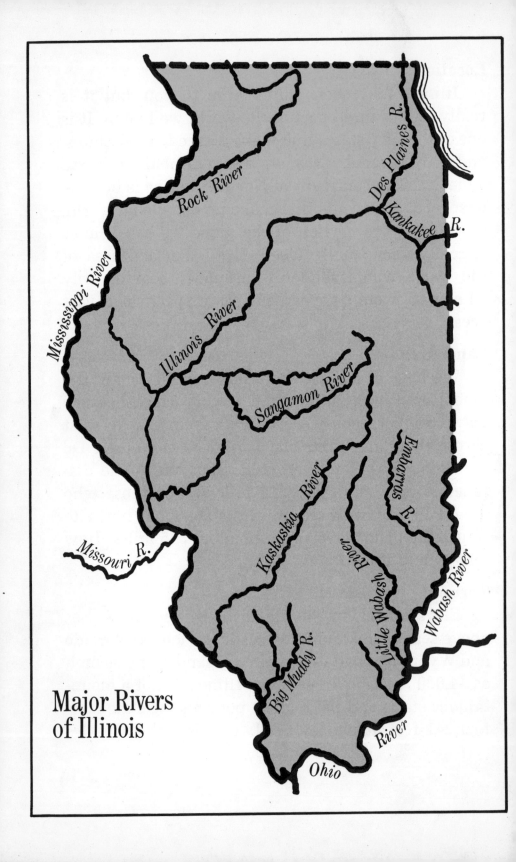

Major Rivers
of Illinois

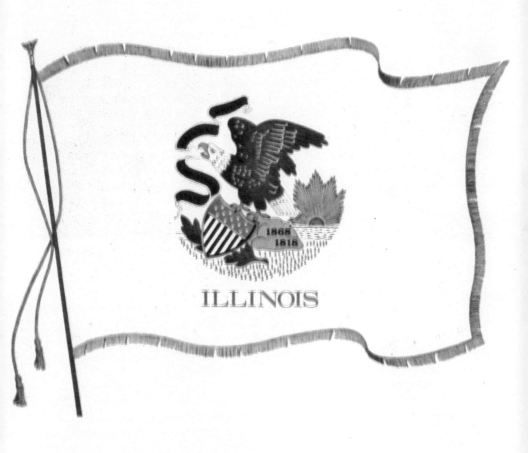

Illinois State Flag was officially altered in July 1970 to more closely resemble the Great Seal and to carry the word "Illinois".

CARDINAL
State Bird of Illinois

NATIVE VIOLET
State Flower of Illinois

FLUORITE
Official Mineral

NATIVE OAK
State Tree of Illinois

The Piasa Bird

The Indians meeting Marquette and Joliet

Abraham Lincoln
The Abraham Lincoln Museum, Springfield

The Liberty Bell of The West

Rotunda of State Capitol

III. Dept. of Business and Economic Development, Div. of Tourism

Historic Galena

Ill. Dept. of Business and Economic Development, Div. of Tourism

Saw and Grist Mill,
New Salem State Park
Springfield News Agency

John Deere Historic Site
III. Dept. of Business and Economic Development, Div. of Tourism

The Rocky Mountains. Where Are They?

Mound and is located in Jo Daviess County. Can you find it on a map of the state?

Do you think people in Colorado or Wyoming would consider this a mountain?

The **terrain** of Illinois is mostly level, sloping gently to the south and southwest where the Ozark Mountains spill over into the state. During the Ice Age, many thousands of years ago, **glaciers** crept down from the north, flattening hills and filling valleys. They smoothed out the land, depositing a rich layer of **alluvial** soil, and molded Illinois into "The Prairie State."

Nearly 85% of the state, or about 30 million acres, is now under cultivation. The wide variety of soil, **climate** and **topography** makes it possible to

WISCONSINAN

GLACIAL

DRIFT

ILLINOIAN

KANSAN
GLACIAL
DRIFT

GLACIAL

DRIFT

The Extent
of Glaciation

grow a wide variety of crops. There is cotton in the **delta** at the **junction** of the Ohio and Mississippi rivers; sugar beets, small grain and vegetables in the north; apples and peaches on the **ridges** where drainage is good; and corn, oats, soybeans, winter wheat, rye and hay found nearly everywhere.

The Illinois Wilderness

Adventurous explorers and pioneers found the frontier land we call Illinois to be a **vast expanse** of beautiful **wilderness.** There were no roads in those days and often only **blazed trails** through the timber enabled people to get from place to place. The many rivers helped early travelers greatly as they provided the means for developing water travel routes.

The only inhabitants of this huge unspoiled wilderness were the various Indian nations and the great numbers of wild animals, such as the bison, deer, mink, beaver and muskrat.

As people came into the area to settle, they changed the appearance of the land. Timber was cleared from much of the land, crops were planted and towns and settlements were built. What had been wilderness slowly turned into a frontier **civilization.**

Climate

Illinois is often referred to as a climate "theater of seasons," with the scene changing four times each year. Each **season** of the year is beautiful in its own way, and many people prefer this variety in climate condition. There are people, however, who dislike one or more of the seasons, or have a season they like best. How do you like the four seasons? Do you have a favorite season?

Illinois is noted for **fertile** land and rich farms. Most of the state has about 35 inches of rain every year, and a short, hot summer, which is good for growing crops. The area at the southern tip of the state has a warmer climate and nearly 45 inches of annual rainfall.

This area is sometimes called "Egypt" or "Little Egypt," and some people believe that this area was named after the great Nile River delta country in northern Africa named Egypt. The capital city of that country is Cairo, and since a city of that same name is located in southern Illinois, and cotton is grown in this region, as it is in Egypt, many believe this to be the reason for calling the area "Egypt."

Historians do not agree with this reason. They say that back in the early 1830s, the northern settlements of the state, due to severe weather conditions, experienced a shortage of corn and meal. Supplies were brought to them from the older and warmer regions in the southern part of the state. It was recalled that in Bible accounts people suffering from **famine** to the north of Egypt were sent supplies of food by that country. The similarity of these actions prompted people of the 1830s to call their area in southern Illinois the "Egypt of North America." How many other similarities can you find between the Egypt in Africa and the area called "Egypt" in Illinois? (Clue: Think about names of rivers, cities, and climate as well as crops.)

Boundaries

The state of Illinois is easily recognized on a map because of its shape. The lines on the map that outline the state are called **boundaries.** These lines are determined usually in two ways:

1. By government survey (man-made or artificial boundaries).
2. By natural terrain features (lakes, rivers, and in some states, oceans).

Which of these kinds of boundaries does Illinois have?

Illinois has a lot of rivers. Altogether there are about 1,277 miles of rivers in the state. Do you know what the longest river is that forms one of the state boundaries? That's right, it is the Mississippi, forming the western boundary. The Ohio and Wabash rivers form the boundary on the southeast side of the state. Can you name five states that border on Illinois? How many are separated from Illinois by a river? The Illinois River is in the center of the state. It begins in the north, where the Kankakee and Des Plaines rivers join, and runs down to Grafton, where it joins the Mississippi. Some other important rivers are the Du Page, Fox, Vermillion, Spoon, Sangamon, Apple, Rock, Kaskaskia and Big Muddy. One is

National Aeronautics and Space Administration

Earth Resources Technology Satellite (ERTS-1) photograph of Chicago area. Can you find: Lake Michigan (upper right corner); Chicago and Waukegan (upper right); Rockford (upper left); Illinois River (lower center); Rock River (left center); Fox River (center); and Joliet (right)?

called the Embarrass, and people pronounce it "Ambraw." Do you live near a river?

The rivers have been important to Illinois. They have provided transportation both for the people and for their products. Can you find these rivers on the map of the state?

The song "Illinois" begins by mentioning rivers. Would you like to learn the state song? You can find it in the data section of this book.

There is another big body of water near Illinois. Do you see what that is on the map of the state? It is Lake Michigan. There are also 352 natural lakes in Illinois and approximately 548 "man-made" lakes, called **reservoirs.** Perhaps you live near a lake instead of a river. Some of the biggest lakes are Bloomington, Crab Orchard, Decatur, Peoria, and Springfield. Which of these is closest to your home?

Scales, Symbols and Legends

Mapmakers, in order to place a great deal of information on a map, must use **scales** and **symbols** to convey meaning or information in as few words as possible. This group of symbols is referred to as the map **legend.** Can you suggest why the term "legend" is appropriate? The mapmaker, by using his legend, makes it possible for anyone looking at his map to identify and locate those things that he has placed on the map. It is a kind of sign language that everyone can read. Study the map legend as shown and try to find out all of the different kinds of information it gives you. Obtain a copy of the Official Illinois Highway Map and try to locate some of the things indicated in the legend.

LEGEND

PRINCIPAL THROUGH HIGHWAYS

MULTILANE DIVIDED, ACCESS FULLY CONTROLLED
MULTILANE DIVIDED, ACCESS FULLY CONTROLLED UNDER CONSTRUCTION
MULTILANE DIVIDED, ACCESS PARTIALLY CONTROLLED
MULTILANE TOLL ROAD
MULTILANE DIVIDED
MULTILANE UNDIVIDED
2 LANE, ACCESS FULLY CONTROLLED
2 LANE, PAVED
UNDER CONSTRUCTION

OTHER THROUGH HIGHWAYS

MULTILANE DIVIDED
MULTILANE UNDIVIDED
2 LANE, PAVED
DUSTLESS
UNDER CONSTRUCTION

OTHER HIGHWAYS

PAVED
DUSTLESS
OTHER ALL WEATHER

ROUTE MARKERS

(80) INTERSTATE
(30) UNITED STATES / TOLL RR
(23) STATE

ACCESS POINTS

FULL TRAFFIC INTERCHANGE
PARTIAL TRAFFIC INTERCHANGE
ACCESS DENIED

3 4 MILEAGE BETWEEN TOWNS AND MARKED ROUTE JUNCTIONS
(12) MILEAGE ALONG ACCESS CONTROLLED HIGHWAY

SPEEDOMETER CHECK SECTION
PERMANENT TEMPORARY
GREAT RIVER ROAD
COVERED BRIDGE
LINCOLN HERITAGE TRAIL
REGIONAL TRAUMA CENTER
STATE PARK, STATE MEMORIAL OR CONSERVATION AREA
STATE INSTITUTION
COLLEGE OR UNIVERSITY
COMMERCIAL AIRPORT WITH SCHEDULED SERVICE
MILITARY AIRPORT
OTHER AIRPORT
ILLINOIS STATE POLICE HDQRS.
OTHER POINT OF INTEREST
REST PARK   REST AREA
PICNIC GROUND OR ROADSIDE TABLE

In congested areas these symbols will generally appear only on the reverse side

POPULATION OF CITIES AND VILLAGES

State Capital
Under 1,000
1,000 to 2,500
2,500 to 5,000
5,000 to 10,000
10,000 to 25,000
25,000 to 50,000
50,000 to 100,000
100,000 and over

County Seats. Population not shown by symbols
In congested areas some municipalities appear only on the reverse side.

0   5   10   15   20   25

SCALE: ONE INCH EQUALS APPROXIMATELY 12 MILES

COPYRIGHT 1973 BY STATE OF ILLINOIS—JANUARY 1, 1973

24

Chapter II

Symbols of the Past

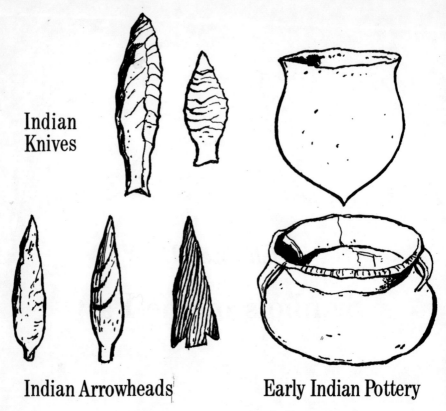

Indian Knives

Indian Arrowheads

Early Indian Pottery

Remnants From Another Culture.

Historic Points of Interest

Have you ever traveled the highways of Illinois and observed the historic site markers along the side of the road? Have you ever stopped to read what these markers have to say on their **inscriptions?** Each of these markers tells about some incident or important happening in Illinois history. Someone has said that these sites are places where history happened.

We have books and other written records of much that has happened in the past, but these written accounts do not go back far enough into the past to

26

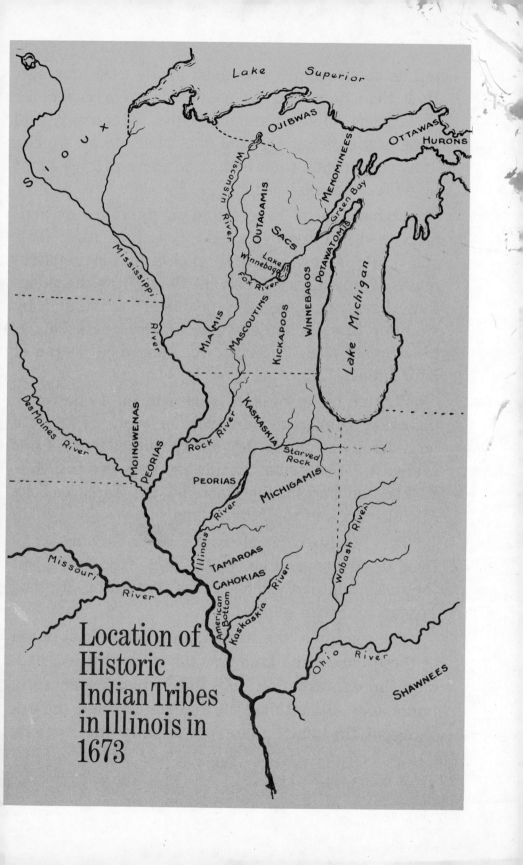

Location of
Historic
Indian Tribes
in Illinois in
1673

tell us about people who lived in the area long ago. How then do we know about these early people? Their story is like a puzzle, to which we can only find some of the pieces. By studying these pieces, we can draw some conclusions and make some guesses about how these people lived.

Archaeologists have found many **relics** or **artifacts** used in these bygone days, such as stone tools and dishes, arrow and spear points, and skeletal remains of animals used for food. Sometimes the skeletons of some of these early people are found and, by studying these, scientists have drawn **conclusions** as to their body characteristics compared to people of later times.

Written history takes us back to the Indian people called Illiniwek. They were only one group of a large family or nation that once occupied most of our Midwest. Other tribes in this family were the Kaskaskia, the Peoria, the Cahokia, the Tamaroa, the Michigamea and the Moingwena.

The Illiniwek people were **seminomadic.** They lived in villages and cultivated some food crops, but they also **migrated** twice a year to hunting grounds in search of wild game.

The coming of the white man had its effect on all of these tribes, and land was taken from them, usually through **treaties** that the Indian never fully understood. Sometimes the Indians resisted the advance of the white man, but usually the settlers,

28

supported by rifles and soldiers, gained control of the land. The Indians either migrated farther north and west or were forced onto **reservations** to live.

What did these people **contribute** to our present-day **culture?** Can you think of anything? You have only to look at a map of Illinois for some clues. The name of Illinois itself comes to us from the Indians. Chicago (Checagou) was an Indian word that some historians say meant great or powerful. Others say that it meant wild garlic or the place where the onion or stinking weed grew. The word "kankakee," after which a city and a river are named, is thought to have referred to the Mohican Indians and meant "wolf." This referred to a particular family or clan of that tribe that used the wolf as a **totem** symbol, and other Indians called them the wolf people.

Kaskaskia, the name given to a river in Illinois, is named after the tribe of that name.

There are many, many Indian names commonly in use in our state today. Look at the Official State Highway Map and see how many Indian names you can find. Does your school, village, city or county have an Indian name?

The Indians had been in Illinois for 10,000 years. Some were very interesting. One group, who lived from 500 B.C. to A.D. 500, was called the Hopewell Indians and they were **mound builders.** When their people died, they buried them and put earth on top. As more people died, the mound got bigger and big-

Illinois State Historical Library

Cahokia Mounds.

Dickson Mounds Museum.

Illinois State Museum

ger. They also buried pottery, weapons and beads with them. You can see the skeletons and the inside of a burial mound at Dickson Mounds State Park near Lewiston.

Other mounds were built as **temples** or for other important buildings by later groups of Indians. The biggest one of these is at Cahokia and is called Monk's Mound. It was built about A.D. 900. Some mounds are in the shape of reptiles, birds and animals. Illinois has about 10,000 mounds, more than any other state. This culture, called Middle Mississippian, was the first to develop the bow and arrow. All of these tribes had **vanished** before any of the early explorers arrived. Can you think of some possible reasons why these tribes might have vanished?

PREHISTORIC INDIANS OF ILLINOIS
A Time Chart
A. **The First Immigrants**

These people are thought to have migrated to North America from Asia by way of Alaska between 30,000 and 50,000 B.C.

B. **The Earliest Hunters**

Discovery sites in the West date from about 35,000 to 6,000 B.C. No occupation sites have been found in Illinois, but many of their spear points have been found here. The earliest Indian village located in Illinois, the Koster site, dates back 8,000 years. This site indicates that they were probably hunters following the herds of big game animals such as the

Aerial view of Monk's Mound, the largest mound in this country and the world's largest prehistoric earthen mound. The base of the mound covers over 14 acres and it is 100 feet high. It was built between 900-1200 A.D., and a large temple once stood on its top, which was probably the home of the "king" or ruler, most likely considered to be a God.

Archaeology students mapping the various layers of dirt uncovered in a mound excavation.

now **extinct** varieties of bison, horse, camel and elephant.

C. Archaic Indians

1. Around the end of the **Ice Age,** about 10,000 years ago, many North American Indians were developing a way of life based on hunting smaller animals and collecting wild plant foods.

2. They lived in small groups and some moved from campsite to campsite on a **seasonal** basis.

3. There are many of these **archaic** sites located in Illinois, but the most important site from which we have gathered information was the Modoc Rock Shelter. Radiocarbon dates obtained from this site run from about 2765 B.C. to 7922 B.C. In digging at this site, archaeologists have found that each inch of soil deposit represents about 50 years of time.

4. These people camped wherever they could find a suitable supply of food and water, and often chose a campsite beneath a large overhanging rock shelter (cliff).

5. Food.

a. Bones of animals, birds and shellfish were found at the Modoc site. From these remains we can guess that they included clams and deer meat in their diet.

b. No remains of buffalo (bison) were found.

c. Remains of now extinct species such as the passenger pigeon have been found, indicating that they, too, were used as food.

6. Tools and ornaments.

a. Tool artifacts found at the Modoc site show that they were usually made from stone and bone. One copper **awl** was found.

b. Many findings included chipped spear points, knife blades, scrapers, stone axes and grinding stones.

c. Ornaments found here included **pendants** and beads made from shell, stone and bone.

d. No evidence was found that would indicate that they had used the bow and arrow at that time. Their main hunting weapon was the spear or javelin, which was thrown by means of a throwing device called the **atlatl.**

e. No pottery was found in the early stages of this site, but some evidence was found in diggings that were identified as about 350 B.C.

D. **Woodland Indians**

1. These people represent a way of life that began about 1,000 B.C. and extended into historic times.

2. They had pottery, and some evidence shows that they grew some plants for food.

3. Religious artifacts show that they had some belief in a life after death.

E. **Hopewellian Indians**

1. These people lived during the period of 350 B.C. to A.D. 350. They were both hunters and collectors of food and cultivated **maize** and other food plants.

2. They constructed large earth works and burial mounds.

3. They lived in villages and had several of these large burial mounds located nearby.

4. They had developed some skills in craftmaking as shown by objects found in these burial mounds. There is evidence that burial tombs were constructed of logs and that these tombs sometimes contained several people, buried with many craft articles of fine workmanship.

a. There appeared to be a kind of cultural **unity** among the Woodland tribes of Illinois, Indiana and Ohio, shown by the similarity of craft artifacts found. It is not known whether there was any form of political (government) cooperation.

b. People of importance buried in these tombs may have been religious leaders, warriors or craftsmen. It is thought that common people (less important) were buried with them or in other cemeteries close by.

c. Hopewellian artifacts have been found in various parts of the eastern United States, indicating that these people may have developed a system of trade between various tribes.

d. Between A.D. 100 and A.D. 350, this culture seemed to **disintegrate,** leaving only smaller, scattered Woodland groups. These continued until what we call the historic period, or that period of time about which we have some kind of written accounts.

F. Mississippian Indians
(A.D. 1000 to Historic Times)

1. The way of life of these people is thought to have developed in the Mississippi Valley, and at its peak spread over large parts of eastern United States. Their culture seems to have been spread among various tribes over a very large part of the country.

2. Their towns or villages were larger than those of other people before them.

3. These people became skilled farmers, and their fields of maize, beans and squash provided much of their food. They were hunters, also, and developed the use of the bow and arrow as a weapon.

4. Two of the more important townsites of the Mississippian people are at Kincaid and Cahokia. Many smaller townsites have been found throughout the state. Dickson Mounds in Fulton County is a large burial ground. Great **pyramids** of earth on which their temples and house of the **council** and chiefs were located were erected around a central **plaza**. The walls of their buildings were poles plastered with clay, and sometimes covered with cane matting. The roofs were usually thatched. The towns were **fortified** with palisades and towers.

5. Farming was their main source of food, and the women did most of the farm work. The men

seemed to specialize in hunting and warfare and did very little work.

6. The Mississippian way of life continued in some parts of the South into historic times. Explorers such as De Soto gave detailed descriptions of some of these tribes. The Cahokia and Kincaid villages were probably **abandoned** about A.D. 1550 to A.D. 1650.

7. The historical connection between the Illini tribes and the prehistoric Mississippian and Woodland peoples, at the time of the French explorers, is not fully understood. It is somewhat of a puzzle, since the Illini tribes seem to have slipped back or lost some of the high achievement of the Mississippians.

EARLY EXPLORERS
Marquette and Joliet

The long birch-bark canoe floated slowly down the river. The two men in the canoe were very tired because they had started their **journey** in Canada. They had to be watchful and wide awake because there might be **hostile** Indians hiding in the trees along the riverbank. They had heard tales, too, of great monsters in the water. They called the river the "Messipi."

These two men were both Frenchmen. They each had their own reason for making the long trip. They had found the northern part of the Mississippi River and were traveling down it, hoping they would find

Illinois State Historical Library

Father Marquette.

Louis Joliet.

a **trade route** to the East. Do you remember another **explorer** who was looking for a trade route to the East? Yes, Columbus, too, wanted to find an easy way to get to the spices and silks and other valuable trade items in the Orient.

One man was a Catholic priest and his name was Father Jacques Marquette (zhak mar ket'). He hoped that he could teach the Indians about his **religion.** The other man was named Louis Joliet (jo le et'). He wanted his home country of France to have control of the land. He also wanted to find good land for the settlers coming from France. Joliet made maps and recorded the animals and birds they saw. He described the kinds of farmland that they passed through, too.

There were five other white men and two Indian **guides** in the other canoes to carry the supplies. The canoes kept floating down the Mississippi River. When they got as far as what is now Alton, they saw two pictures of monsters painted on the rock cliff by the river. They were afraid, because they knew that the Indians must have painted the pictures. Father Marquette wrote in his diary that the monsters were as big as a calf, with horns on their heads like those of a deer, a horrible look, red eyes, a beard like a tiger's, a face somewhat like a man's, a body covered with scales and a tail so long that it winds all around the body, passing over the head and going back between the legs, ending in a fish's tail. It was painted

40

red, green and black. This was later to be called the Piasa Bird or Thunderbird (pie uh saw).

Marquette and Joliet turned their boat around and started back toward the north. They had figured out that the Mississippi would continue to the **Gulf** of Mexico. How did they know? (The river was getting wider and the **current** was faster.) They knew that they weren't going to find the **Orient**. They were the first two white men in what is now Illinois, when they turned their canoes and headed up the Illinois River. The year was 1673.

Can you find the Illinois River on the map? Do you see where they turned into it from the Mississippi?

They passed Indian villages along the Illinois River on their way north. Six tribes, the Kaskaskia, Peoria, Michigami, Tamaroa, Cahokia, and the Moingwena, had banded together and were called the Illini **Confederation**. Illinois is the French way of saying this tribe's name.

The Indians were friendly to Marquette and Joliet. They stopped to visit one tribe who lived between what is now Ottawa and La Salle.

The Illini lived in **dome-shaped** lodges. They were covered with reed mats woven by the women. Sometimes four or five families lived in one lodge.

The women of the tribe did the farm work. They raised corn, beans, melons and squash and picked berries. The men hunted deer, bear and buffalo with

Illinois State Museum

In this museum diorama an Indian chief greets Marquette and Joliet.

Indian "Wickiup" or dome-shaped house, covered with reed mats.

Illinois State Historical Library

their bows and arrows. They trapped beaver and fished in the streams. The Illini always had plenty of food.

The Illini chiefs wore red scarves made of the hair of bear and buffalo. They painted their faces red when they went to war with other tribes. The Illini could be very mean and **warlike** sometimes. When they took prisoners from the other tribes, the women and children were often kept as slaves.

The Illini men had several wives. If a wife **disobeyed** her husband, the husband might cut off her ears or her nose. Marquette wrote that he had seen women who had **misbehaved** and therefore had their faces **disfigured.**

The most important thing to an Illini warrior was his peace pipe or **calumet.** It had a wooden stem two feet long with a red polished stone to hold the tobacco. It was decorated with the heads and necks of various birds. When Marquette and Joliet left the Illini, the Indians gave them a calumet to help protect them on their journey.

One of the chiefs and some of his men led Marquette and Joliet up the Illinois River to Lake Michigan. They went to where Evanston is today. (Can you find it on a map?) Marquette and Joliet promised to come back again and build a church for them.

Marquette became ill, but he still kept his promise to the Indians. He came back at Eastertime, in 1675, and built the first mission or church in Illinois,

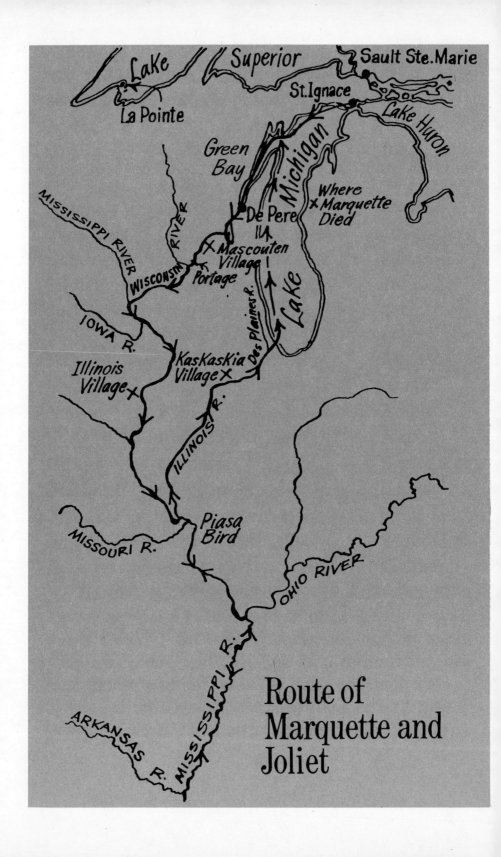

Route of
Marquette and
Joliet

Sieur de La Salle.

Illinois State Historical Library

Henri de Tonty.

for the Illini, by Starved Rock, near Ottawa. Joliet never returned to Illinois, because his government wouldn't give him permission.

Father Marquette and Louis Joliet had a successful **voyage**. They found out that the Mississippi River ran all the way down to the Gulf of Mexico. They also found out that the Indians were friendly. Marquette established a **mission** for his church in the new land. Joliet thought that the prairie land would be good for farming and would help to bring **settlers** to Illinois. Was he correct in his thinking?

La Salle and Tonty

When the news of Marquette and Joliet's successful trip reached Canada, two more Frenchmen started for the Illinois country. They wanted to build a long line of **forts** from the Great Lakes to the Gulf of Mexico to collect all of the Indians' furs. The leader was named Rene Robert Cavalier, and his title was Sieur de La Salle (da la sal'). The other man was Henri de Tonty, called Iron Hand by the Indians because he had a hook for a hand which had been lost in a battle in Europe. The Indians had never seen a man with just a hook for a hand.

On January 5, 1680, their first fort was built near Peoria on the Illinois River. The French called it Fort Creve Coeur (krev ker'), which means Fort Heartbreak. This was the first non-Indian occupation of the region that is now Illinois. La Salle returned to Canada for supplies and left Tonty in charge.

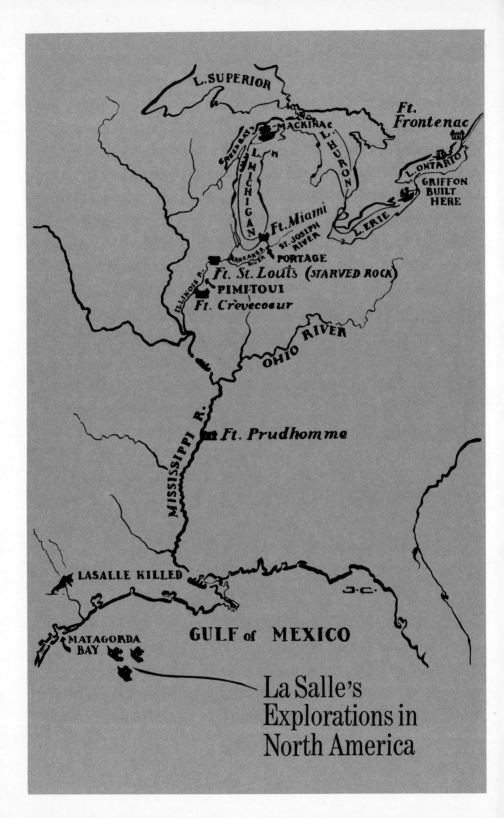

La Salle's
Explorations in
North America

Tonty had trouble with his men and with the Indians, and had to leave the fort and head north, too. The fort was burned to the ground.

When Tonty and La Salle got together again two years later, they followed the Mississippi River down to the Gulf of Mexico and claimed all of the land along the river for France. They returned to the Illinois River and built a fort by Starved Rock, where Marquette and Joliet had visited, and called it Fort St. Louis after the king of France. La Salle again left Tonty in charge of the fort.

La Salle went to France, and when he returned by ship, he tried to find the **mouth** of the Mississippi in Louisiana. He got lost and ended up in Matagorda Bay in Texas. La Salle and his men set off on foot for Illinois, but the men got so angry with him for his mistake, that they murdered him in 1687.

This time, though, Tonty got along better. He moved the fort called St. Louis back down to Peoria. He asked for settlers to come into the valley and for **missionaries** to come and start churches. He worked on setting up **trading posts** to bring in supplies and take out the furs. By the time Iron Hand died in 1704, his dream had come true. The fur trade was going well and forts were built from Canada to the Gulf of Mexico.

Another fort, called Fort de Chartres (da shart'), was completed in 1720, near Prairie du Rocher (da row'shur). The Mississippi River flooded many times

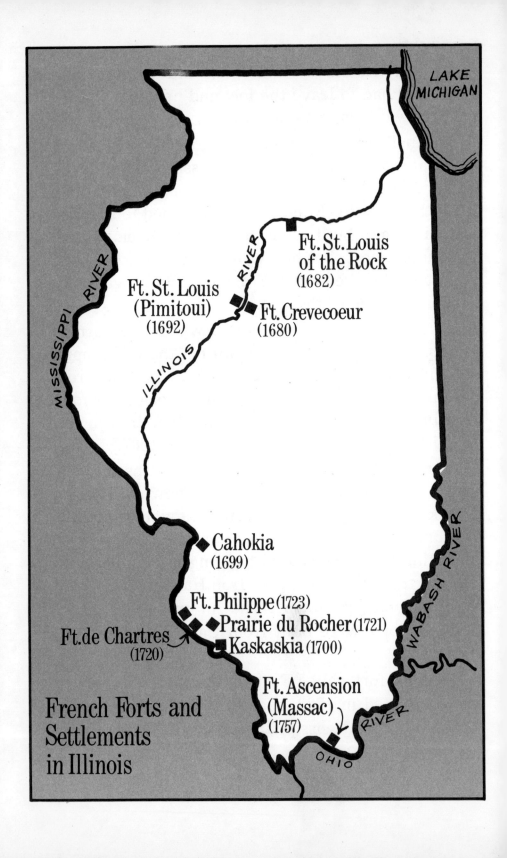

LAKE MICHIGAN

MISSISSIPPI RIVER

RIVER

Ft. St. Louis
of the Rock
(1682)

Ft. St. Louis
(Pimitoui)
(1692)

Ft. Crevecoeur
(1680)

ILLINOIS

Cahokia
(1699)

Ft. Philippe (1723)

Prairie du Rocher (1721)

Ft. de Chartres
(1720)

Kaskaskia (1700)

WABASH RIVER

Ft. Ascension
(Massac)
(1757)

RIVER

OHIO

French Forts and
Settlements
in Illinois

Early French Settler's House.

and washed under the walls. The fort had to be replaced in 1756, and the builders thought that they had the best and strongest fort of all. It was the pride of France and they made it the seat of government for the Illinois country.

Some of the missionaries who came to the Illinois country built a church south of present East St. Louis in 1699. It was where the Tamaroa Indians spent their summers. The little town that grew up around the church was called Cahokia (ca hoe kee a). Can you find Cahokia on a map? This was the first permanent **settlement** in Illinois since the Tonty forts were **abandoned** and then started up again. Cahokia is also the oldest town in Illinois.

51

In four years the church was moved farther south to another Indian village. These Indians were called the Kaskaskia, and that is what the priests called their town.

All the people in these first Illinois settlements were French and Catholic. The church played a very important part in their lives. The people were happy and got along well with the Indians. They farmed, growing a lot of wheat and other grain, which they traded for **supplies.** It is interesting to see the Frenchmen's houses. They put the logs up and down rather than across like the log cabins we usually think of. They loved to dance and sing.

In 1754, the British and French began a long war over the land in the Ohio and Mississippi river valleys. Both sides wanted the Illinois country. They also wanted the Indians to be on their side and to help them. Most of the Indians remained **loyal** to the French, whom they knew and had worked with. This war, which ended in 1763, is known as the French and Indian War. The French lost the war and lost the Illinois country. The British became the new rulers of Illinois. How would Illinois have been different if the French had won? What language would you be speaking?

In October 1765, the British finally took over Fort de Chartres. The name of the fort was changed to Cavendish and a new flag was flown over it. The

French had lost the fort, but the guns were never fired. The strong fort was never tested.

But the English soldiers had trouble. The French people didn't like them and neither did the Indians. A lot of the French moved across the river to St. Louis, Missouri, to get away from the English. The English used Fort Cavendish until 1772.

The Potawatomi, Ottawa and Chippewa tribes were on the **warpath** against the English. They wanted the French trappers back in power instead of the English, who brought settlers that took over Indian lands. Pontiac, chief of the Ottawa, had been murdered in 1769, in Cahokia, when he came to talk. A Peoria Indian hit Pontiac on the head and stabbed him to death. The three tribes came south from the Detroit area to get their **revenge.** The Illini ran to the top of the big rock by their home. They were safe up there, but their food and water soon ran out. They tried to let buckets down into the Illinois River to get drinking water, but the warring tribes cut the ropes. When the Illini tried to sneak down off the rock to get food, they were killed. Most of the Illini died of starvation, and that is supposedly how Starved Rock got its name.

George Rogers Clark

A lot of settlers had come to America by the 1770s. People in the 13 **colonies** had decided that they wanted their **independence** from England. One man, named George Rogers Clark, had an idea. He

Starved Rock.

thought that he could get the Illinois country away
from the English and give it to Virginia. Governor
Patrick Henry of Virginia said that Clark could try.

George Rogers Clark gathered up an army of
175 men and set out for Kaskaskia, the seat of the
English government at that time. It was the 4th of
July, 1778, when they arrived. Clark was 26 years
old. The people were friendly to Clark and wanted
to get out of English control, and he took over the
town. Then he thought that perhaps he should go
back across the Illinois country to Vincennes. (It is
now in Indiana, but it was a French settlement at
that time.) The French people there told Clark that
they would rather become Americans, too.

George Rogers Clark.

General George Rogers Clark leads his men through the flooded Ohio to attack the British at Vincennes, in February, 1779.

The English wanted to recover Kaskaskia and Vincennes. About 600 English soldiers came down from Detroit and took Vincennes back for the English. Then most of them went back to Detroit because winter was coming and they thought that the Americans wouldn't be able to fight in the winter. But George Rogers Clark fooled them.

In February of 1779, Clark set out from Kaskaskia. It was very cold and wet, and 240 miles to march to Vincennes. About 170 men agreed to go with Clark. The Indians called them the **"long knives"** because that is what they carried.

The women helped, too. They made 20 American flags so that the people in Vincennes would think

56

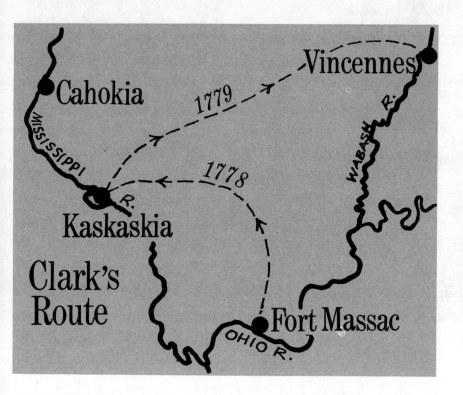

Clark's Route

a lot more soldiers were coming. Clark and his "long knives" surprised the small British force and captured Vincennes. It was a very important victory. Otherwise this whole area might have been kept by the British as a part of Canada. Can you think how life here would be different if it had become a part of Canada? Would our government be different? Would we celebrate the 4th of July?

The people in Virginia were very happy with what George Rogers Clark had done. When the 13 colonies got their independence from England after the Revolutionary War in 1784, they also got the

During the French and Indian War the Illinois Indians siding with the French fired on canoes carrying British troops.

Northwest Territory. This included all the land west to the Mississippi River. Was Illinois part of this? Virginia gave her right to the Illinois country to the new federal government.

Illinois now had another flag flying. The first flag was Spanish because Columbus had claimed all of the country for Spain when he discovered America. Then Marquette and Joliet claimed the land for France. The British flag was next after the French and Indian War, and now, at last, the American flag.

Settlers weren't afraid of the Indians or war any more, so they decided to move west to Illinois where land was available at a low cost. The settlers came by **flatboat** and by **covered wagon.** Most of the people stayed along the rivers. There were usually trees near the rivers to use to build their houses. Sometimes, when there were no trees, they used stones and dirt for their houses. These were called **sod huts.** Another reason for settling by the rivers was that when the trees were cut down, more land was cleared for farming.

The boats that came up the rivers brought in supplies. The water in the river was used for power to turn the **mill wheel.** There were flour mills and sawmills.

In 1800, the Northwest Territory was divided and the Illinois country was made a part of the Indiana Territory. Nine years later Illinois became a separate territory. Ninian Edwards was the territorial governor. He later became one of the first senators from Illinois.

The settlers were a brave and rugged group. The Americans again went to war with England in the War of 1812. The Indians could see that many settlers were arriving and making their homes on Indian lands. The Indians fought on the side of the British in the War of 1812, trying to win the land back from the settlers. One battle was won by the Indians at Fort Dearborn, what is now Chicago. It was just a fort in the wilderness at that time, and the Indians killed most of the people at the fort. There would be more Indian fighting in the northern part of Illinois, but the Indians moved from the land in southern and western Illinois at about this time. More and more settlers moved in to claim the land and soon the entire territory was covered with many small settlements or early towns.

Chapter III

ILLINOIS' PEOPLE

Palestine

Edwardsville

Illinoistown
Carlyle
Cahokia
Belleville
Palmyra
Bellefountain
Albion
Mt. Carmel
New Design
Waterloo
Prairie du Rocher
Carmi
Kaskaskia
Major
Settlements
Brownsville
Equality
in Illinois by
Shawneetown
Elvira
the end of 1818
Jonesborough
Golconda

Population Density

Illinois has grown steadily from a wilderness frontier to the **populous** state that we know today. There were fewer than 2,500 people in Illinois by the year 1800, and by the year 1850, there were about 851,000. This figure grew to over 3,800,000 by 1890, and by 1920 the figure had increased to over six million. Why do you think the population grew so rapidly during this period from 1800 to 1920?

Early population centers, about 1800, were established at Cahokia (719), Kaskaskia (467), Prairie du Rocher (212), and Bellefontaine (286), while southern St. Clair County had only 250 residents. Monroe County had about 330. There were also about 100 living in the Fort Massac area and fewer than 100 French fur traders scattered over the entire area.

The population of Illinois, by the 1970 census, is 11,113,976, and is composed of many **races** and **nationalities** from all over the world. The major center of population is now the Cook County **metropolitan** area, which has 5,492,369 people, or nearly half of the entire state's population. Can you name other area population centers in Illinois today?

Cities and Towns: Population Symbols

Did you ever consider a road map to be anything but a highway location device? It is really a book of information and there are many things you can learn by being able to read this book. It is not an ordinary book, for instead of having pages of words, it makes use of a system of symbols to give information. If all the information contained on a common road map ~~~ *- ha ~--* into writing it would probably contain more pages than the book you are reading now.

Do you know what kinds of information you can get from a road map? What did you learn about map scales and symbols in Chapter One? Most official highway maps have a legend or symbol explanation box to tell you what each symbol represents. In this chapter we will study the symbols that represent cities and towns and will try to find out what the mapmaker has to tell us about these places.

The official highway map of Illinois is issued by the Illinois Department of Transportation (try to obtain a copy for your study) and uses the following symbols to give information about cities and towns:

O Small towns under 1,000 population.
◎ 1,000 to 2,500 population.
◓ 2,500 to 5,000 population.
● 5,000 to 10,000 population.
⊣◇⊢ 10,000 to 25,000 population.
⊣◇⊢ 25,000 to 50,000 population.
⊣◉⊢ 50,000 to 100,000 population.
⊣●⊢ 100,000 and over.
✪ State capital.
⊙ County seats.

Find these towns on the Official State Highway Map:

Chatsworth is indicated by the symbol ◎. What does this tell you about Chatsworth? Weldon is indicated by this symbol ○ . What does that tell about Weldon? Fairfield is indicated by this symbol ◉. What does this tell about Fairfield? Vienna is indicated by this symbol ⊙ . What does this tell about Vienna? Sometimes a city will be indicated by two symbols. Charleston is an example. Can you find the two symbols for Charleston? What does each symbol tell you?

What symbol does your city or town have (or one close to you, if you live in a **rural** area)? The map also tells us how to quickly locate any city or town in the state. The Illinois **index** to cities and towns is arranged alphabetically and shows the latest population figures after each name. Can you find this index to cities and towns on the Official Highway Map of Illinois?

Following the name and population figure, a number and a letter are given. Do you know what they mean? Notice that across the top and bottom of the map are the numbers 1 to 10, at two-inch intervals. From top to bottom on both sides of the map are the letters A to P, also spaced two inches apart. This gives a **grid** location system that may be used to locate any city or town listed in the map index. What county seat town in Illinois is located by the grid 5A? What county is this town located in? Locate

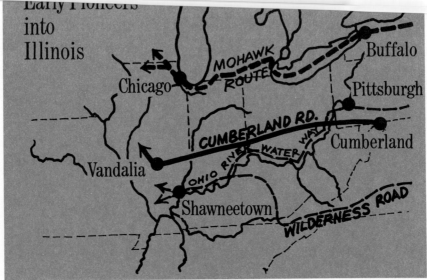

Routes of
Early Pioneers
into
Illinois

MOHAWK ROUTE

Buffalo

Chicago

Pittsburgh

CUMBERLAND RD.

Cumberland

OHIO RIVER WATER WAY

Vandalia

Shawneetown

WILDERNESS ROAD

your own town or city with the grids given in the map index.

Where the People Came From

Earlier we learned that Illinois was once a wilderness and that many people came here to make their homes. In this chapter we have looked at the towns and cities where most of the people live. Let us now consider where these people came from (or their parents or grandparents). Where did they live before and why did they choose to come to Illinois?

Illinois is often referred to as a "melting pot," which means that many different races and nationalities came into the state, became neighbors and friends, and shared common interests and **goals** so that they all became known as "Illinoisans." Remember, the American Indians were the first or original Illinoisans. They were forced from the land into other areas as the other races came into the state.

The first wave of **immigrants** came into the state in the 1800s, and was composed mostly of people from northern Europe and the British Isles. The population grew, and by 1818 the Illinois Territory became a state in the United States family of states. Indian treaties opened up more land for settlement in the Midwest, and railroads were built, making travel easier.

Workers were needed in lumbering and for railroad building, and the demand for crop and livestock products grew rapidly. Immigration reached its **peak** in the 1850s, when there was a growing need for workers in canal and railroad building. These people came from Ireland, and by 1860 there were four times as many Irish in Chicago as in the rest of the state. Some people from Germany also came for construction jobs, but most of the Germans were farmers or **tradesmen.** German settlements came into being near St. Louis and in downstate areas at Alton, Belleville, Galena, Peoria and Quincy.

Two groups of people from Portugal settled at Springfield and Jacksonville. French Canadians migrated to the Kankakee River area, and such towns as Kankakee, St. Anne, Momence and Chiniquy were

Early Nauvoo.

started. People from France came and settled in Chicago and downstate, where they opened stores and shops. The Mormons established a large, prosperous settlement at Nauvoo, but were later forced to leave the state because of religious differences. Was this the first time people had been forced to leave Illinois? (Remember the Indians?)

The **Scandinavians** avoided the cities and opened new land to farm. The first Norwegian settlement was near Ottawa, on the Fox River, and a later settlement was established near present-day Norway, Illinois.

The French and English had come to Illinois even before it was a state. After Illinois became a state

Early settler prairie "dug-out."

Painting by Olaf Krans, renowned artist-resident of Bishop Hill settlement.

(1818), people came not only from other parts of the United States, but from other countries as well. Some of the people were farmers and some had other

people from one country all gathered in one town. The Swedish people, for example, gathered in Rockford and Moline.

One group of people, who also came from Sweden, started a town called Bishop Hill in Henry County. The Swedes had become angry about the lack of **freedom** in their homeland, so they came to America, where they could **worship** as they pleased. The first winter they lived in caves dug into the ground. The next summer they built their homes. All the people worked together. Some of the women cooked the food for everyone; other women watched the children or did the laundry. They worked for the group instead of for themselves. This is called **communal living.**

A group of Englishmen settled in Albion. These people also came to Illinois hoping for a better life in the new country of America. The planners of this town, George Flower and Morris Birkbeck, had the cabins waiting for the first fifty settlers. They encouraged the settlers to come to "English Prairies." Why do you think they called it that?

All of these people had trouble getting used to the new land, because their dress, **customs** and language were different. Usually, when the children

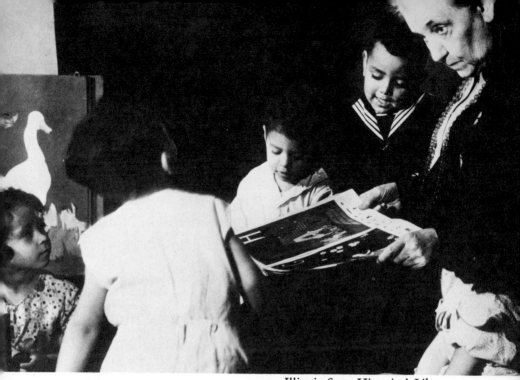

Jane Addams and her settlement house children.

Hull House.

went to school, they learned English. This helped them to become a part of the new land. Can you

be difficult?

Not all the people who came to Illinois stayed. Many pushed on west to settle in Iowa, Nebraska and Kansas. Still others followed the Oregon Trail to California and Oregon.

Over the years people have come to Illinois from all over the world. There are many Chinese in Chicago, as well as Italians, Germans, Poles, Irish, Russians and Mexicans, to name a few.

In 1889, Jane Addams opened Hull House in Chicago. This was a **settlement house.** Chicago had many immigrants or strangers from other lands. They didn't know how to speak English or how to get along in their new country. The settlement house was a place where they could go to learn English, to find new friends and to meet neighbors from their homeland. Jane Addams won the Nobel Peace Prize for helping and serving others during her life.

The black man has been in Illinois since 1720, when the first slaves were brought here by Philipe Renault to work in the salt and lead mines. One slaveowner, Illinois' second governor, Edward Coles, freed his slaves as he crossed into Illinois on the Ohio River. He had come from Virginia, a slave state.

Governor Coles freeing his slaves on the Ohio River.

He gave each of the newly freed men 160 acres of land.

One black man, named Frank McWorter, manufactured saltpeter and earned enough money to purchase his own freedom, and soon that of his wife and children. Can you imagine buying your freedom?

William de Fleurville, another black man, had the first barbershop in Springfield and was Abraham Lincoln's barber. A black Chicago doctor, Daniel Hale Williams, performed the first successful heart operation. Many black men have served in the legislature and courts of the state of Illinois. There are also famous black people in the arts, such as Gwen-dolyn Brooks, the poet laureate of the state of Illi-

Here is a short poem by Gwendolyn Brooks called "Pete at the Zoo."

I wonder if the elephant
Is lonely in his stall
When all the boys and girls are gone
And there's no shout at all,
And there's no one to stamp before,
No one to note his might.
Does he hunch up, as I do,
Against the dark of night?

The "Chicago Daily Defender" and magazines like "Ebony" and the "Negro Digest" are published in Chicago.

Illinois was the first state to **ratify** the 13th Amendment **abolishing** slavery. **Segregation** has been forbidden in the public schools since 1874, and an 1885 civil rights act forbids **racial discrimination** in restaurants, hotels, theaters, railroads, streetcars, and places of public accommodation.

Someone has said that if you were to stick a pin into any country on the globe, there would be some people from that country (or their descendants) in Illinois. Red, yellow, black or white, the melting pot of Illinois has taken all and produced a culture rich from the **contributions** of all.

Where did the people come from? They came

74

from all over the world. Where did your family originally come from? Can you tell from a person's name where his family came from?

Special Customs and Celebrations

Culture is made from custom and **tradition,** and passed from one **generation** to the next. Language, clothing, religious belief, games, recreation, **festivals,** food and many other things go into the making of a culture, and when people leave one area and settle in another, they take these things with them. What happens when people from many culture backgrounds all move into the same geographic area? Some parts of their old culture die out and they adopt some new characteristics in their place. For example, the English language has almost replaced all other languages brought by different nationalities to Illinois. Clothing style has changed to reflect the view of the new area. Some cultural **traits** of one group are accepted by all groups and become a part of the new culture. Music is one example of this.

Do you know which nationality group contributed polka music to our culture? A new culture is formed then by taking on parts of all the cultural traits of the various nationality groups that live in the same geographic area, in this case the state of Illinois.

Some cultural customs and celebrations have not died out and are preserved through regular observance by various nationality groups. Let us look at some of these cultural observances in our state.

Where	What	
Norris City	Frontier Days	May
Arcola	Rail Splitting Days	May
Metamora	Old Settler's Festival	June
Geneva	Swedish Days	June
Silvis	Mexican Fiesta	July
Jacksonville	Prairieland Heritage Festival	July
East Moline	Greek Festival	August
Rock Island	Indian Powwow	August
Nauvoo	Wine and Cheese Festival	August
Springfield	Illinois State Fair	August
Gifford	German Fall Festival	September
Rockford	Oktoberfest	September
Altamont	Schuetzenfest	September
Ingleside	St. Bede Festival	September
Petersburgh	Fall Festival	October

The above list tells only a few of the hundreds of events and observances held in Illinois each year. If you would like to find out about others, you might write to the following address and request the Illinois Calendar of Events:

Illinois Department of Business
and Economic Development

Division of Tourism
222 South College Street
Springfield, Illinois 62706

Culture and Heritage

The history of Illinois is rich in people and events. The frontier has long vanished in Illinois, but annual festivals celebrate our **heritage** and life as it was. Community **centennials,** pioneer days, county fairs, jamborees and jubilees renew the arts, crafts and way of life from bygone eras when German, French, Swedish, and Amish pioneers first settled on the Illinois prairie.

Proud of this heritage, some 100 museums, monuments and memorials across the state trace Illinois' change from an **agrarian** society to an industrial economy. Remnants from various periods of history are preserved in many ways—from roadside markers to the incredible Field Museum of Natural History in Chicago. Sites like William Bryan's birthplace in Salem, Governor Woods' home in Quincy and Galena's Market Place have been preserved through state and local efforts. The state museum in Springfield traces the highlights of Illinois' history with unique **dioramas.**

Statehood

So many settlers had come to Illinois by 1817 that there were over 40,000 people in the territory. Most of these people lived in the southern part of the ter-

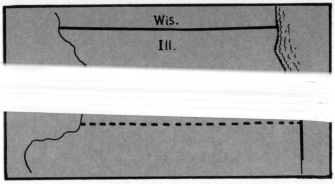

The 41 additional miles that Nathanial Pope's amendment added to Illinois' northern boundary.

ritory in small one-room log cabins on the prairie. When the people gathered together, they talked about becoming a state. Ohio, Indiana and Mississippi had just become states and it seemed like a good idea for the Illinois Territory as well. Nathaniel Pope was chosen to go to Congress and speak for the people back in Illinois Territory.

The people of Illinois played a trick on Congress. They didn't have quite enough citizens. They needed 60,000. A **census** was taken to count the people, but it was done so slowly that Illinois was made a state before the counting was finished.

Nathaniel Pope did some smart thinking and added land on to the north. Illinois was supposed to be just as far north as Indiana, just at the bottom of Lake Michigan. Do you see that on a map? Nathaniel Pope wrote an **amendment** asking for 41 more miles. The 41 miles were added so Illinois would have a **port** on Lake Michigan. If he hadn't done that, Chicago and 14 other counties would have been part of

78

MAP OF
ILLINOIS
SHOWING
COUNTY BOUNDARIES
1818.
(ILLINOIS TY.).

Wisconsin. Would your county have been part of Wisconsin?

———— .... wrote a constitution. Congress an-

the papers and Illinois ......
day was December 3, 1818. Illinois was the 21st state of the United States. The capital was Kaskaskia.

Examine our United States flag. Each star represents one state. How many stars are in our flag today? How many states do we have now? Can you find the star for Illinois?

Shadrach Bond was elected the first governor. Ninian Edwards and Jesse B. Thomas were elected senators. John McLean was the state's first representative. Illinois was off to a good start. Do you know who the governor is now? Do you know your senators' names? What is your representative's name?

Look at the map which shows some major settlements in Illinois by the year 1818. Do you see that only the southern part of the state was settled? There are now 102 counties in Illinois. Do you know the name of your county?

An Illinois City in 1877

In 1877, Freeport had a population of 9,013 people. The county had been in existence for about 40 years and the city had received its charter 22 years before. Since Freeport was the **county seat**, the courthouse and jail were located there. There were four grade schools, one high school, fourteen churches, three newspapers—one in German, called "The Deutscher Anzeiger" (German Advertiser)—and one hotel. The growing town had the usual supply of doctors, lawyers, dentists, bankers, veterinarians, grocery stores and clothing stores. It also had some other businesses that aren't around today. This is a list from the Freeport City Directory of 1877-78.

Agricultural Implements — Smyth, W. R. B., Agent for McCormick's reapers and mowers

Blacksmiths—Geo. Mernitz

Boardinghouses—H. C. Bray

Breweries—Albion Ale, Freeport Brewery, Western Brewery

Brickyards—Freeport Brick Co.

Bridge Builder—F. E. Josel: Patentee of Josels Iron and Wood Bridge

Broommaker—Wm. Hilder

Buffalo Robes—Reineke and Otto

Carpets and Oilcloths—William Walton

Carriage Manufacturers—J. L. Robinson and Co.

Cement and Stucco—Bering and Perkins

Churn Manufacturer—W. P. Emmert

Cigar Manufacturers and Dealers—Jacob Krohn

Coal Dealers—Geo. Bordner

Coopers—Wm. Braun

Coppersmiths—Arndt and Leemhuis

Crockery—D. Franz and Son

Currycombs—Reineke and Otto

Dressmakers—Mrs. D. T. Carver

Door Spring Manufacturer—L. A. Warner—Warner's celebrated "You Git" door spring

Express Company—American Express Co.

Fly Nets—D. B. Schulte
Fresco Painter—Daniel Adamson

Horse Collars—Reineke and Otto
Horseshoers—Ligget and Gibler
Insurance Companies—28 listed, and Freeport is still
    prominent in the business
Lime Kiln — Bering and Perkins — perpetual lime
    kiln
Livery Stables—Bergman and Dorman
Marble Works—Bissel and Petitt—sell everything in
    the marble line
Milliners—Mrs. C. C. Wilson
Music Teachers—Mrs. C. Hammell
Omnibus Lines
Patent Medicines—Emmert and Burrell
Rag Carpets—Allmendinger and Bender
Saloons—29 listed
Schoolbooks—Mrs. C. Baumgarten
Sewing Machine Agents—C. C. Wilson sells Howe
    Sewing Machines
Shoemakers—Herman Wachendorf
Soda Water Manufacturers—Galloway and Snooks
Spectacles—A. W. Ford
Spring Beds—D. Kuehner
Stair Builders—Waddell Bros.
Steamship Agents—American Steamship Line,
    White Star Line
Stoves and Tinware—Burchard and Scott
Telegraph Institute—Western Union
Trunks and Valises—James McNamara
Undertaker—D. Kuehner

Some Early Day Luxuries

Vacuum Oil Blacking—Reineke and Otto
Vinegar Works—Chas. E. Meyer

Well Driller—D. D. Wareham
Whips—Reineke and Otto
Windmills—Winger and Devore
Woven Wire Mattresses—D. Kuehner

Could Mr. Reineke and Mr. Otto make a living today? What other businesses would be in trouble today? Where do you think most of the settlers in Freeport came from? What other businesses would we need today?

Illinois in Abraham Lincoln's Time

The favorite son of Illinois is Abraham Lincoln. We call our state the "Land of Lincoln" in his honor. Illinois claims Lincoln even though he was born in Kentucky. He also lived in Indiana before he came to Illinois with his father and stepmother. He was 21 years old in 1830, when he first saw Illinois. It was in Illinois that he became **famous.**

The family went to Decatur to build a cabin near their relative, John Hanks. The Lincoln family moved again the next year to a cabin near Charleston, but Abraham decided to be on his own. He was a poor boy who had only about one year of school.

Lincoln decided to go to New Salem. He had seen the town the year before from a raft when he had taken farm products down to New Orleans to sell.

84

The Lincoln Trail State Memorial across the Wabash River from Vincennes, near U.S. Route 50, commemorates Abraham Lincoln's arrival in Illinois, in 1830, at the age of 21.

Lincoln got a job running a store for Denton Offut. He knew he had to get more schooling, so he read all the time. When customers came to the store, they always found him reading. In the summer he sometimes lay on his back under a tree, with his long legs stretched up the trunk. He read all the books that he could find or borrow. A book about the life of George Washington was one of his favorites.

In 1832, the Offut store was closed, and Lincoln **enlisted** to serve in the Black Hawk War. The other

Black Hawk.

86

soldiers elected him captain. The settlers in northern Illinois were in a **panic.** They thought Black Hawk and his Sac and Fox Indians [...] sacre the settlers. The reason [...] had led his people back to lan[...] where the tribe had lived long ago. Do you see the Rock River on a map?

The state officials said Black Hawk had no right to be in Illinois, since the Sac and Fox had given up their lands by treaty and had agreed to move across the Mississippi into Iowa. Black Hawk replied that the white men had **bribed** the chiefs, and the Indians hadn't really understood what they were doing. Who do you think was right?

In 1812, Black Hawk had fought with the British. When the British lost that war, Black Hawk had to return to his tribe without getting back the land of his people.

In 1831, the Sac and Fox were still living in Illinois, and Governor John Reynolds told Black Hawk to move across the Mississippi. Black Hawk agreed. He asked the Potawatomi, Winnebago, and Mascouten Indians for promises of help, and the next year moved back into Illinois from Iowa. Governor Reynolds then called for **volunteers,** and the Army sent some troops, too. When all the soldiers appeared, the other tribes **deserted** Black Hawk.

Between the spring and fall of 1832 there was a number of **clashes** between the soldiers and In-

Bad Axe Battleground

Prairie du Chien

WISCONSIN R.

MISSISSIPPI R.

MICHIGAN TERRITORY

Galena

Apple River Fort

BLACK
HAWK'S
TRAIL

Rock Island

Black Hawk Village

Yellow Banks

KELLOGG'S
TRAIL

ILLINOIS RIVER

Beardstown

ROCK RIVER

Stillman's Run

Dixon's Ferry

ILLINOIS

Chicago

Indian Creek
Massacre

SAUK TRAIL TO CANADA

Peoria

The
Black Hawk
War

dians. Abraham Lincoln was with the volunteers, but did not take part in the fighting. Jefferson Davis, who later became president of the Confederate States during the Civil War, was a lieutenant in the army.

General Henry Atkinson led the pursuit of the Indians, and when they fled into Wisconsin, he defeated them at the Battle of Bad Axe, on the Mississippi River. It was more of a massacre than a battle, for the Indians had tried to surrender. It is not considered a proud moment in our history.

Black Hawk was captured and placed in the care of Jefferson Davis. A treaty was signed at Fort Armstrong, and the Sac and Fox Indians agreed to leave Illinois forever and live in Iowa.

There were still a few Indians of other tribes living along the northern border of Illinois, and the settlers wanted to get rid of them, too. The next year, after the Black Hawk War, the government called all of these Indians to Chicago. Several thousand Indians took part in the council and signed a treaty giving up all their lands west of Lake Michigan to the Mississippi. The Indians agreed that within three years they would all move west of the Mississippi River, and the government agreed to give them money to build houses and mills; to pay teachers, doctors and blacksmiths; and to make cash payments to the chiefs. The final payments were made at a second meeting in Chicago in 1835. After that meet-

The Lincoln burial services.

ing the Indians danced a **mock** war dance through the streets of Chicago. It was the last appearance of the Indians in their former homeland of Illinois.

When Lincoln got back to New Salem after the Black Hawk War, he again tried to run a store. The store failed, and he lost his money, and then was made postmaster. Next he tried **surveying.** He entered politics and was defeated for a try as a legislator in 1832, but he tried again and won in 1834. He was a state legislator for six years.

After Illinois became a state in 1818, the capital was moved from Kaskaskia to Vandalia, offering a more central location and not subject to periodic flooding such as the Kaskaskia location. In 1837, Lincoln joined with eight other legislators to get the

POSTVILLE
COURT HOUSE SITE
FROM 1839 TO 1848 THE SEAT
OF LOGAN COUNTY WAS
POSTVILLE, WHICH CENTERED
IN THE COURT HOUSE
LOCATED ON THIS SITE.
IN THIS STRUCTURE
ABRAHAM LINCOLN, A
MEMBER OF THE TRAVELING
BAR OF THE EIGHTH
JUDICIAL CIRCUIT, ATTENDED
COURT TWICE A YEAR.
ERECTED BY THE STATE OF ILLINOIS
1934

Illinois Division of Tourism

capital moved again. They were called "The Long Nine" because they were all over six feet tall. Lincoln was six feet four. "The Long Nine" worked hard, and finally on February 25th of that year, got the capital moved to Springfield. It was nearer the center of the state. You can visit the old state Capitol in Springfield and see it just as it looked when Lincoln was serving as a legislator in the building. Springfield is still the capital of the state of Illinois. Lincoln moved to Springfield from New Salem on April 15, 1837.

After serving in the legislature, Lincoln decided that he wanted to be a **lawyer.** He worked first in

Springfield with John Stuart, then he joined Stephen T. Logan, and finally formed his own law firm with William H. Herndon. He was considered one of the best lawyers in Illinois. He traveled all over the area, going to Mount Pulaski, Metamora and Postville courthouses to handle **cases.** Many people got to know him.

Abraham Lincoln married Mary Todd in 1842. They had four boys. Three of them died when they were quite young. Only Robert lived to manhood.

In 1846, Lincoln was elected to the House of Representatives and went to Washington, D. C. He was not re-elected two years later. By 1850 the population of Illinois had grown to 850,000.

One of the leaders in the fight over **slavery** was Elijah Lovejoy. He was a white newspaperman who had been run out of Missouri and had brought his printing presses to Alton. He printed antislavery literature. A mob got together to destroy the "Alton Observer." Elijah Lovejoy was killed by the mob as he tried to defend and save his printing presses.

His brother, Owen Lovejoy, played an important part in the **"Underground Railroad."** This wasn't a railroad at all, but just a house or barn where the Negroes were hidden during the day. They were sent on the next night to the next safe hiding place. This continued until the black family was safe from the slaveowner or people who sold slaves back into slavery.

A farmer hides a family of runaway slaves in his barn, a station on the underground railroad.

In 1850, Illinois, like all the other states, was concerned about slavery. When Illinois was made a state, the Northwest Ordinance had **forbidden** slavery. Also the first constitution forbade slavery. There were some slaves in Illinois though. They had been here before the laws were passed. Even the "free" Negroes had few rights. No new Negroes were allowed into the state. Sometimes men from slave states would come to Illinois and capture "free" Negroes and take them back to the South and sell them into slavery. Other people were trying to help the slaves by taking them to the North where they could be free. Illinois was **divided.** The people in southern Illinois were mostly from the South, where slavery

93

was permitted. They were "for" slavery. The people in northern Illinois were mostly from the East, where slavery was forbidden. They were "against" slavery.

The Republican Party was formed by those people who were against slavery. Lincoln joined this new party and decided to run for the Senate against Stephen A. Douglas in 1858. They agreed to have a series of seven **debates,** one in each congressional district. The towns chosen were Ottawa, Freeport, Jonesboro, Charleston, Galesburg, Quincy and Alton. Many people came to hear them discuss the slavery issue. Lincoln argued that the nation couldn't be half slave and half free. It is said that Lincoln was the best debator, but Douglas won the election. People all over the United States read and talked about the debates.

In 1860, Lincoln and Douglas were two of the **candidates** for President of the United States. Lincoln was **nominated** in Chicago in a wooden building called "the wigwam." This time Lincoln was the winner. He became the 16th President of the United States.

The Southern states were very upset about the slavery issue. They decided to form their own government and not be a part of the United States. This started the Civil War. Illinois sent 259,092 men to fight in the war. There were many famous generals and men from Illinois. General Ulysses S. Grant be-

Illinois State Historical Library

Lincoln debating Douglas at Charleston.

The Republican "Wigwam" where Lincoln was nominated for president.

Illinois State Historical Library

Civil War Union Prison Camp at 35th Street in Chicago.

came the leader of the entire Northern army. Other generals from Illinois were John A. Logan, John M. Palmer, John Pope, Stephen A. Hurlbut, Elon H. Farnsworth, Michael Lawler and Richard Oglesby.

Illinois lost 34,834 soldiers in the Civil War. A man from Belleville, Senator Lyman Trumbull, drafted the 13th Amendment to the Constitution, which forbids slavery in the United States. Illinois was the first state to **ratify** this amendment.

The war lasted until April 9, 1865, when the South finally surrendered.

On April 15, 1865, Abraham Lincoln died. He had been shot by John Wilkes Booth while watching a play. All the people in the North were sad. His body was brought home to Illinois by a funeral train.

The Lincoln Monument.

People all the way from Washington to Springfield watched and cried as the train went past. Lincoln was buried in Springfield. Today his wife and three sons are buried there beside him. His fourth son, who lived to be an old man, is buried in Arlington National Cemetery in Virginia.

The Wit and Wisdom of Abraham Lincoln
Selected Quotations

"I don't know who my grandfather was," Lincoln once said. "I am much more concerned to know what his grandson will be."

"My father taught me how to work, but not to love it," Lincoln said. "I never did like work and I admit it. I'd rather read, tell stories, crack jokes, talk, laugh—anything but work."

In settling a debate on how long a man's legs should be, Lincoln declared, "It is my opinion . . . that a man's lower limbs in order to preserve harmony of proportion, should at least be long enough to reach from his body to the ground."

Lincoln once said of his countenance, about which many people poked fun and ridicule, "In my poor, lean, lank face nobody has ever seen that any cabbages were ever sprouting out."

When writing letters to his friend John Addams, who ran the mill in Cedarville, Lincoln would start his letters, "My Dear Mr. Double D Addams." There is a story, too, about when he married Mary Todd;

he said that one D was enough for God, but that it took two D's for Todd.

There is an interesting anecdote told about Lincoln's campaign for Congress. He attended a religious camp meeting, where his opponent, Peter Cartwright, was the speaker. Mr. Cartwright was a circuit-riding Methodist preacher, and he said to the audience, "All who desire to give their hearts to God and go to heaven, will stand." A sprinkling of men, women and children stood up. Then he said, "All who do not wish to go to hell will stand." All stood up, except Lincoln. "May I inquire of you, Mr. Lincoln, where you are going?" Lincoln rose and said, "I am going to Congress."

The Famous House Divided Speech

In a speech made before his famous debates with Stephen Douglas, Lincoln had this to say about slavery:

"A house divided against itself cannot stand. I believe this government cannot **endure** permanently half slave and half free. I do not expect the Union to be **dissolved** . . . I do not expect the house to fall . . . but I do expect that it will cease to be divided. It will become all one thing, or all the other. Either the opponents of slavery will **arrest** the further spread of it . . . or its **advocates** will push it forward till it shall become alike lawful in all the States, old as well as new, North as well as South."

In defending his thinking to friends who cautioned him that such a view could mean failure for him politically in the upcoming Douglas debates, Lincoln said, "If it is decreed that I should go down because of this speech, then let me go down linked to the truth . . . let me die in the advocacy of what is right and just."

Lincoln's Farewell to Springfield, February 11, 1861

The Illinois State Journal of February 12, 1861, reported "despite bad weather . . . hundreds of his fellow citizens, without distinction of party, had assembled . . . to bid him God-speed." After silently shaking hands with many of his well-wishers, the President-elect and party boarded the train. Shortly before eight o'clock, on the platform of the rear car Lincoln bared his head to the rain, faced his friends, and stood silently struggling with his feelings . . . then slowly, solemnly spoke . . .

My Friends—

No one, not in my situation, can appreciate my feelings of sadness at this parting. To this place, and the kindness of these people, I owe everything. Here I have lived a quarter of a century, and have passed from a young to an old man. Here my children have been born, and one is buried. I now leave, not knowing when, or whether ever, I may return, and a task before me greater than that which rested upon Washington. Without the assistance of that Divine Being, who ever attended him, I cannot succeed. With that assistance I cannot fail. Trusting in Him, who can go with me, and remain with you and be everywhere for good, let us confidently hope that all will yet be well. To His care commending you, as I hope in your prayers you will commend me, I bid you an affectionate farewell.

(The original draft of the above version is in the Robert Todd Lincoln Collection of the Papers of Abraham Lincoln, now in the Library of Congress. The Springfield Illinois State Journal version is on a plaque in the Lincoln Tomb. After the train pulled away, Lincoln wrote down a few sentences of his Farewell and it was then completed by John G. Nicolay, his private secretary.)

The Gettysburg Address

(These are the remarks made by President Lincoln at the dedication of the National Cemetery at Gettysburg, Pennsylvania, November 19, 1863.)

Four score and seven years ago our fathers brought forth upon this continent, a new nation, conceived in Liberty and dedicated to the proposition that all men are created equal.

Now we are engaged in a great civil war, testing whether that nation, or any nation so conceived, and so dedicated, can long endure. We are met on a great battlefield of that war. We have come to dedicate a portion of that field, as a final resting place for those who here gave their lives, that that nation might live. It is altogether fitting and proper that we should do this.

But, in a larger sense, we can not dedicate —we can not consecrate—we can not hallow

—this ground. The brave men, living and dead, who struggled here, have consecrated it, far above our poor power to add or detract. The world will little note, nor long remember, what we say here, but it can never forget what they did here. It is for us, the living, rather, to be dedicated here to the unfinished work which they who fought here, have thus far, so nobly advanced. It is rather for us to be here dedicated to the great task remaining before us—that from these honored dead we take increased devotion to that cause for which they here gave the last full measure of devotion—that we here highly resolve that these dead shall not have died in vain—that this nation, under God, shall have a new birth of freedom—and that, government of the people, by the people, for the people, shall not perish from the earth.

Second Inaugural Address

In March of 1865, upon taking office for his second term as president, and with the end of the Civil War in sight, Lincoln's thoughts turned to the **reuniting** of the nation. From that speech came this famous quote: "With **malice** toward none; with **charity** for all; with firmness in the right, as God gives us to see the right, let us strive on to finish the work we are in; to bind up the nation's wounds; to care for him who shall have borne the battle and for his widow, and his orphan—to do all which may achieve and cherish a just and lasting peace among ourselves, and with all nations."

Chicago as first settled by Jean Baptiste Point du Sable (at right), showing his first cabin (at left).

Chicago in 1892.

Chicago Through the Years

The early Indians had villages along Lake Michigan. A mission was set up there by Father Pierre Pinet for the Indians in 1696. It was along a river that the Indians called "Checagou," which means strong or mighty in the Indian language. Neither the French nor the English had ever started a town by Lake Michigan.

In 1779, a black man named Jean Baptiste du Sable arrived from Canada and built a log cabin. He traded with the Indians. Du Sable married a Potawatomi woman and had to travel 280 miles down to Cahokia to find a Catholic priest to marry them.

The Du Sables worked hard and built up the trading post. They also farmed the land and ran a flour mill. There was no other place within 200 miles where a traveler could get meat, bread, or supplies.

When Du Sable sold the land in 1800, he had two children and a well-established trading center. He moved to St. Charles, Missouri, where he died in 1818. So, you see, the "Father of Chicago" was a black man.

A fort named for Henry Dearborn, the Secretary of War of the United States, and called Fort Dearborn, was built on the site of Chicago in 1803. It was completed after the United States had signed the treaty with the Indians. Some settlers arrived and

Fort Dearborn, 1803.

settled near the fort so that the soldiers could protect them.

On August 15, 1812, the fort was threatened by an Indian attack. Instead of the people staying in the fort, they tried to run away. Most of the children, 2 women, 12 **militia,** and 26 regular army men were killed by the Indians. All the rest were captured except one family. Only the Kinzie family escaped. They were good friends of the Indians. This was called the Dearborn Massacre. A new fort was built in 1816.

More people came to Chicago in the next 20 years. By 1833, there were about 200 people and Chicago became a town. The Erie **Canal** had opened in the East so that boats could come through the Great Lakes. Can you see the Great Lakes on a map? What

Tug used in construction of the Illinois and Michigan Canal.

The Chicago fire in 1871.

are their names? How many are there? Are any of them completely in the United States? The people in the rest of the state of Illinois sent their agricultural products to Chicago for shipment back to the East. The settlers left their boats at Chicago. They needed a place to stay and transportation for the rest of their journey overland. Chicago was going to help them.

Two things that helped Chicago grow were the Illinois and Michigan Canal and the Galena and Chicago Union Railroad, which began operation in 1848. Chicago had become a city in 1837, and it was growing fast. Wooden buildings were going up and board sidewalks were being built. Ships, trains and people were all busy.

Remember, Abraham Lincoln was nominated for president in a wooden building in Chicago in 1860. Do you remember the name of that building?

Chicago played an important part in the Civil War. Horses, mules, and products made in the new **factories** helped to supply the soldiers. These products were all shipped out of Chicago.

The summer and fall of 1871 had been hot and dry. The wind was blowing hard. The story goes that a fire started when the cow Mrs. Patrick O'Leary was milking kicked over the **lantern.** (Why didn't she have the lights on?) The wind blew the flames and soon the whole city of Chicago was on fire. All the wooden buildings and sidewalks burned. The fire

107

lasted for 27 hours—from Sunday night, October 8, through Monday, October 9. It was so hot that some of the people waded into the lake, and still their hair caught on fire. Others packed up what they could in their wagons and carried things in their arms to try to get away from the fire. When the fire was over, 17,450 buildings, including 1600 stores, 28 hotels and 60 factories had been destroyed. When the fire was out, 90,000 people were homeless and 300 were dead.

Fire Prevention Week that you observe at school always includes the date of October 9, to commemorate the Chicago fire.

The people started to rebuild Chicago as soon as they could. This time they didn't use wood. They used **masonry** and stone to construct the new city.

In 1885, William LeBaron Jenney's Home Insurance Building made history. It had upright steel **beams** and steel floors with an outer "skin" to cover them. Then a 22-story Masonic Temple Building was built using the same pattern. It was built by Daniel Burnham and John Root. With this new type of construction, the **architects** and builders could make the buildings as tall as they chose. Chicago architects had invented the **"skyscraper."** Chicago is still a leader in building skyscrapers. The Marina Towers look like two corncobs. The Hancock Building, nicknamed "Big John," or "Big Stan," the Standard Oil Building, and the Sears Building are all examples. They are some of the tallest buildings in the world. Have

Chicago Association of Commerce and Industry
Chicago today.

you ever seen a skyscraper? Do you have a skyscraper in your town?

Chicago has had three great fairs. One was in
1893. It was called the Columbian **Exposition** to
celebrate the discovery of America, 400 years before.
A lot of people came to see Chicago for the first time.
The fair was held to present to the world the progress made in manufacturing, trade, and the arts.
They also rode on a ride that had just been invented,
called the "Ferris wheel." Have you ever seen a
Ferris wheel? Have you ridden on one?

The people also saw the tall buildings. They saw
a city rebuilt after the fire. The fair was held in

Jackson Park, and all the buildings were white. Chicago was nicknamed "the White City."

Miss Lura Eyestone of Bloomington, many years later, gave her impression of how she was warned not to try the Ferris wheel, but her curiosity won out and she tried it anyway. Miss Eyestone, in 1963, could still remember the thrill of the ride. She had boarded the train in Bloomington, about four o'clock one July morning, to go to the fair. She was accompanied by two older ladies, and they stayed in a hotel on the south side of the fair.

She fondly remembered the art building, the Japanese building, the Mexican building, and, of course, the Ferris wheel. Shortly after she rode the Ferris wheel, it stopped, and it took several hours to repair it. One of the newer things at the fair was an optometrist's stand where people could get their eyes tested. Miss Eyestone found that she had "long distance viewing." What does this mean?

Her biggest complaint concerned the high prices of food: coffee, 10 cents; soup, 15 cents; steak, 80 cents.* Because these prices were so high, many people lived on the free samples distributed at the fair, went outside the gate and got a ham sandwich for 5 cents, or brought a picnic lunch.

This fair, held in what is now Jackson Park, attracted about 28 million people, with a daily average

---

*Baumgart, Jackie. "The White City Fair," *Illinois History,* October 1963, pp. 10-11.

of over 150,000. There were about 150 buildings and **exhibits** from all over the world. It was a turning point in American life, for it opened the eyes of Americans to the beauty and culture of many lands. Most world fairs are still modeled on the Columbian Exposition held in Chicago at the close of the 19th century.

In 1933, Chicago had a birthday party for being 100 years old. There were more new buildings along the lake front. Some of these buildings were unusual shapes and colors and all were lighted by electric lights. The exhibits included new developments in science, industry, agriculture, transportation, **electronics,** communications, and home planning. Chicago was still growing, with all of the hustle and bustle of a big city.

The International Trade Fair was held in 1959. This fair was to celebrate the opening of the St. Lawrence Seaway. This meant that the biggest ships in the world could come through the Great Lakes to Chicago. It also meant that Chicago was an ocean port even though it wasn't on the ocean. Can you find the St. Lawrence Seaway on a map? Have you been to Chicago? Did you see big **ocean liners** and **freighters** in the **harbor?**

Today Chicago is still growing. Old buildings are often torn down to make room for newer, modern buildings. What had once been the site of a little Indian village sitting in a vast wilderness has now

Chicago Association of Commerce and Industry
Photo by Kee T. Chang

Chicago, a city of skyscrapers rising from the prairie.

become one of the major cities of the world. Instead of a few hundred Indian residents, it now has millions of people who live there. What do you think Chicago will be like by the year 2000?

Turn to the Data Section of this book and find additional information about Chicago. (Hint: Try looking in the Data Section under the topic "Manufacturing in Illinois.")

Chapter IV

Education and Communication

The Northwest Territory
Showing the year each state was admitted

Early Education

Schools were slow to develop in Illinois because most of the early pioneers were not interested in book learning. They preferred the **practical** education of life on the **frontier.** However, the early Protestant preachers spread learning while they spread the **gospel** among the settlers.

The first school was begun by John Seeley in 1783, using an abandoned log cabin. Seeley operated the school on what is called a **subscription** basis. That is, he collected whatever he could in money, supplies or services from the parents of his students. Seeley's teaching covered what have been called the three R's: reading, 'riting, and 'rithmetic. How does this education compare with your education today?

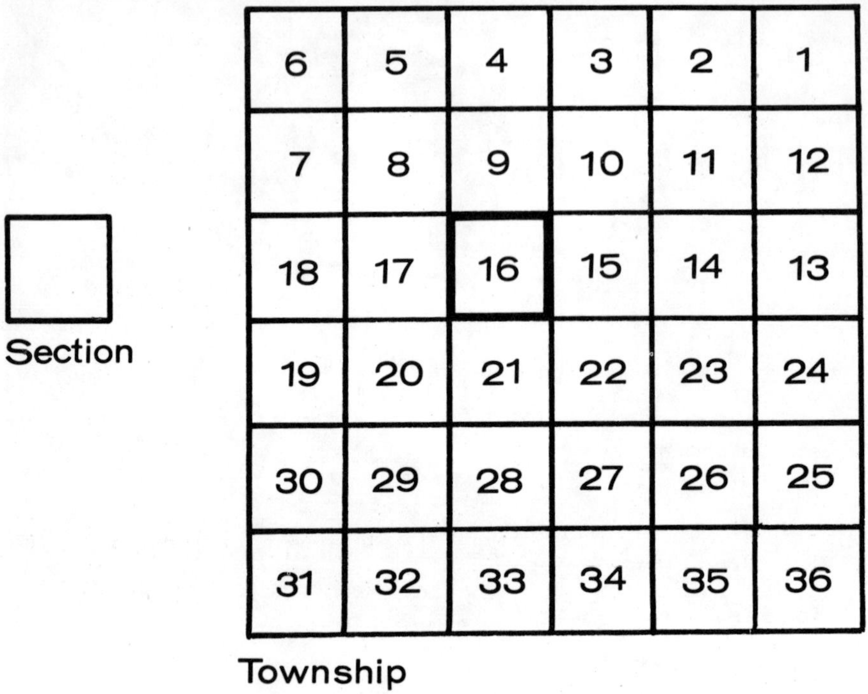

6	5	4	3	2	1
7	8	9	10	11	12
18	17	16	15	14	13
19	20	21	22	23	24
30	29	28	27	26	25
31	32	33	34	35	36

Section

Township

Township and Section Plot.

There were only a few scattered schools like Seeley's in Illinois when, on July 13, 1787, Congress passed an **ordinance** governing the old Northwest Territory, of which Illinois was a part. This ordinance gave some encouragement to education by providing that, "Religion, **morality** and knowledge being necessary to good government and the happiness of mankind, schools and the means of education shall forever be encouraged."

When the government **surveyed** the new land, it divided it into one mile square **sections.** Thirty-six of these sections made up a larger unit called a **town-**

ship. The enabling act reserved section 16 of each township, along with the state's salt springs, for the use of schools. Can you think of a reason for choosing section 16?

Nathaniel Pope, Illinois' territorial **delegate** to Congress, also persuaded the national lawmakers to set aside for education 3 percent of the money from the sales of **federal lands** in the state. One sixth of this was to go to colleges and universities and the rest to schools.

In reserving section 16 of each township for schools, Congress set aside some 998,448 acres. However, there were already settlers on some of this land and they preferred to buy their farms rather than rent them. So, the school lands were sold and the money **invested** in banks in the state. Some of this money was lost when these banks **folded.** Some of the school money was also **borrowed** by the state to pay other expenses.

A step toward making up these losses was taken by a law prepared by State Senator Joseph Duncan and passed by the state legislature in 1825. This law allowed the counties to raise a small **tax** to educate children between the ages of five and twenty-one. The state also provided some tax money for the schools and five sixths of the **interest** due on the school money it had borrowed. However, the settlers were not yet ready to pay a school tax and the law was **repealed** four years later.

A second school tax law was passed in 1836 and signed into law by Joseph Duncan, who was now governor. Only a few **free schools** were started under this law. The first had begun in Chicago in 1834. Others followed in Alton in 1837, and in Springfield and Jacksonville in 1840.

Jacksonville was also the site of the first free public high school in Illinois. This was the West Jacksonville District School organized by Newton Bateman in 1851. Until then parents had to pay to send their children to high school, just as they now pay to send them to college.

By 1854, the friends of education in Illinois had persuaded the state legislature to **create** an independent, elected post of Superintendent of Public Instruction. The first superintendent, Ninian W. Edwards, was **appointed** to the job on March 15, 1854. Edwards drew up a school tax law which required the counties to support free schools. This law passed the legislature in 1855, and the first statewide free school system began in Illinois.

The first college in the state to begin classes was Illinois College in Jacksonville. Construction of this college's first building began in 1829, and Professor Julian Sturtevant began teaching the first class of nine students in the still unfinished building on January 4, 1830. This building, Beecher Hall, is still in use on the Illinois College campus.

Like the other colleges in the state at that time,

Beecher Hall, first building on the Illinois College campus at Jacksonville.

Illinois College was for men only. The first college for women in Illinois, Jacksonville Female Seminary, opened in Jacksonville in 1833. In 1903, the **seminary** merged with Illinois College.

Illinois' first state university was the last of the great Midwestern state universities to begin full operation. It was **chartered** as the Illinois Industrial College at Champaign-Urbana in 1867, and opened in March of the next year. It received the state's share of **federal funds** provided by the Morrill Act, which granted government land for a university to provide education in agriculture, engineering and other mechanical fields. In 1885, the Industrial College's name was changed to its present name, the University of Illinois.

University of Illinois

University of Illinois in Champaign-Urbana, the Illini Union building.

University of Illinois, Champaign-Urbana, the Assembly Hall.

University of Illinois

The university received little state help until Governor John Altgeld began his term in 1893, then it began a rapid growth. The university broadened its program to cover other areas of education. Today there are over 32,000 students and 3,000 teachers on the Champaign-Urbana **campus,** and nearly 23,000 more students, and nearly 2,000 more teachers, on two campuses in Chicago.

Our Schools Today

Illinois schools today are very different from the log cabin schools like John Seeley's. The fireplaces and later wood-burning stoves which roasted those close by while those farther away shivered, have been replaced by modern **central heating.** The benches made of logs split in half, have been replaced by modern desks and study tables.

The early schools had few books, so the students brought whatever they happened to have at home. Usually this was a Bible, which had to serve as a reading **primer.** Do you think it would have made a good one?

Today even the poorest schools have books covering a variety of subjects for several different grade levels. Many schools even have libraries, or **media centers,** which hold not only books, but movie films, tape recordings and records as well. How many of these different things does your school have?

Even in the rural areas, schools today have several rooms, but until after 1947, schools like this

Diorama showing the interior of early, one room schoolhouse.

Students and teachers of early one room school.

were found only in the cities and towns. In the country, in 1947, many children still went to one-room schoolhouses where one teacher taught all eight grades. Perhaps your grandparents can tell you what it was like to attend such schools.

School buses today **transport** to their classes children who live more than a mile from school. In the cities other children often ride the city buses to school. However, before the buses were invented many students had to walk, often several miles, to school. Some rode horses and kept them in **sheds** on the school grounds. Can you imagine a lunch period in which a student would have to feed both himself and his horse?

While many of the early pioneers did not care for book learning, many later settlers viewed education as a **privilege.** How do you feel about your education today?

In the early days many students, especially boys, had to drop out after the eighth grade. This was not always because they could not afford to go to high school, but because they were needed to help out in the fields. Also many school terms were set to begin after the fall harvest and end before the spring planting season, so that younger children could also help out on the farms during these busy times. Is this expected of you today?

Many of our high schools today provide their students with the opportunity to train for a wide

RULES AND REGULATIONS

FOR THE GOVERNMENT OF THE

PUBLIC SCHOOLS

IN THE CITY OF DECATUR.

1 All Children between the ages of five and twenty-one years, who reside in the School District, have a right to the privilege of the Public School.

2 No pupil shall be allowed to attend School, unless furnished with the Text Books and Stationery, as required.

3 Any pupil who has been exposed to, or who is afflicted with any contagious disease, shall not attend School until all danger of contagion is removed.

4 No pupil shall leave one School to attend another, without the written consent of the Directors.

5 Regular and Punctual Attendance is required of every pupil; and for repeated absence or tardiness, say, for the space of four half days in two successive weeks, such pupil shall forfeit his or her seat, unless they shall present a written excuse from the Parent or Guardian, stating such absence to have been caused by sickness, or other unavoidable circumstances.

6 No pupil shall leave School before the hour of closing, without permission of the Teacher.

7 No pupil shall be absent from any Examination of the School.

8 Every pupil shall pay for all damages he or she may do to the School Building or Furniture, or the property of other pupils, and may be suspended until payment is made. Nor shall any pupil use or write profane or unchaste language in or about any of the School Buildings, or in any manner deface the Public School property.

9 All Books, Papers, Periodicals, or Novels, having no connection with the School Studies, are prohibited from being brought into the School.

10 Pupils are strictly forbidden to engage in Play or Sport, within the Halls or Rooms of the Building, unless under the direction of their Teacher; nor shall they enter the Adjoining Lots of Citizens, or in any way injure or disturb their property.

11 All Pupils shall promptly and respectfully obey their Teachers.

12 In the Morning the Principals shall be at the School Room twenty minutes, and other Teachers and Pupils fifteen minutes before the time of commencing School. In the Afternoon, all Teachers shall be in their respective places at the Ringing of the Bell, five minutes before the time of commencing School. The hours for commencing School, shall be, punctually at Nine O'clock in the Morning, and half-past One O'clock in the Afternoon.

13 Teachers will be required to teach six hours in each day; and no recess or intermission shall be given for a longer time than ten minutes.

14 Any Scholar wilfully violating any of the foregoing Rules and Regulations, may be suspended by his or her Teacher, until the next meeting of the Directors.

15 Any person feeling aggrieved in reference to any matter connected with the School, the cause of such grievance must be stated, in writing, to the Directors, if action is desired thereon.

Decatur, Illinois, September 10th, 1860.

Wm. E. NELSON,
D. L. BUNN,
LOWBER BURROWS,
}Directors.

Printed at the "Illinois State Chronicle" Book and Job Printing Office, Water Street, Decatur.

Figure 13, Illinois History Documentary Series, No. 2

Illinois State Historical Society

Early Public School Regulations.

variety of **occupations.** Those who are interested in agriculture, home economics, business, or the building trades can learn the **skills** they will need to begin work in these fields. Others who want to become engineers, doctors, lawyers, teachers, or enter other professional fields can take courses which will prepare them for college or university study. To help students decide which occupation they wish to follow, some high school **counselors** are arranging for the young people to talk to those who are engaged in various occupations in their communities.

Colleges and Universities

There are thirty-eight private colleges and universities in Illinois, ten colleges and universities run by churches, and eight state universities. The origins of these colleges date back to 1828, when the first pioneering efforts to establish colleges in the state were begun. In each case the new college or university was formed in order to improve the educational opportunities in Illinois either in general or in some **specialized** field of learning.

The colleges and universities required money, devotion, sacrifice and effort from their **founders.** Continuing higher education in Illinois still requires these qualities on the part of the present-day supporters of colleges and universities. Money, and how best to use it, is usually the only requirement that poses as great a problem today as it did for the pioneers in education. However, even this can be overcome as it has been many times in the past.

None of the private or church-supported colleges receives any aid from the state, except, of course, these colleges pay no taxes. The private colleges rely mostly on gifts from earlier **graduates,** business and industry and **tuition fees.** The church-related colleges get most of their support from the **denomination** itself, with some other money from the same sources as the private colleges.

One of the big problems for the large state universities is finding room to grow. Some have solved this by building **high-rise** buildings. Northwestern University, however, found a different approach. It filled in part of Lake Michigan with two million cubic yards of sand to make the site for its new James Roscoe Miller campus.

Junior Colleges

Many graduates of Illinois high schools do not wish to enter a full four-year college either because of the expense or for other reasons. Yet their chosen **careers** require more training than they have received in high school. For these students there are many two-year community or junior colleges in Illinois. In these colleges the students can either take courses that will prepare them to transfer to a four-year college or university later, or they can take courses that will train them in special skills in just two years.

Of the forty-five junior colleges in Illinois, nine are private and the rest are operated either by state, county or **municipal** governments. These are all part of a project to make every school district part of a junior college district. When this is completed, students in Illinois will have the opportunity for a **tax-supported education** from grade school through the first two years of college. Thus, the goal set by State Senator Joseph Duncan in 1825, of providing an education for students from age 5 to 21, will finally be accomplished.

Which of the state junior colleges is closest to where you live?

Turn to the data section of the book and see what other information you can find about education in Illinois.

State Historical Society

It took four tries to establish the Illinois State Historical Society. The first three, in 1827, 1837, and 1843, failed because the organizations lacked public and private **financial support** and the members found it difficult to attend meetings because of travel conditions. By 1899, a network of railroads had linked all the towns and communities of the state. So the **trustees** of the Illinois State Historical Library, which had been established in 1889, called a meeting at the University of Illinois on May 19, 1899, to **establish** an historical society.

Hiram W. Beckwith, a Danville attorney and

author, was elected the society's first president, and Evarts Boutell Greene, a history professor at the university, was elected secretary. On May 23, 1900, the Illinois State Historical Society was chartered by the state as a **not-for-profit corporation.** The General Assembly made the society a department of the Illinois State Historical Library on May 16, 1903.

Can you imagine a building which has two stories above ground and three below ground? Well, this is what the home of the Illinois State Historical Society is like. The two stories above ground are the Old State Capitol, which served as Illinois' fifth statehouse from 1840, when Lincoln was a state legislator, until 1876.

When the state government outgrew the building, it was sold to Sangamon County, which used it as a courthouse. In 1899, the building was extensively remodeled, including jacking it up and adding a new first floor. The state bought the building back in 1961 and **reconstructed** it as it had been in 1840. On December 3, 1968, it was **rededicated** and presented to the State Historical Society by Governor Otto Kerner. The society now operates the Old State Capitol as an historic site.

The square on which the Old State Capitol sits has also been **landscaped** to look as much as possible like it did in Lincoln's time. Underneath the square, however, things are nothing like they were in the 1840s. There you will find the three-story Illinois

State Historical Library surrounded by a two-level parking garage.

The thick walls of the library keep any of the noise and **fumes** from the cars in the parking area from entering. In fact, elaborate heating and air conditioning on the lowest level of the library carefully control the temperature, humidity and **air quality** inside the library. This protects the library's extensive collection of books, pamphlets, magazines, manuscripts, **microfilms,** and so forth from any harm. These materials cover the history of Illinois, Abraham Lincoln, and the Civil War, and include many one-of-a-kind items.

In 1972 the library's holdings included:

125,906 books and pamphlets.

1,278 broadsides (sheets of paper especially of a large size, printed on one side, for distribution or posting).

3,307,024 manuscripts.

849 maps.

2 motion picture reels.

1,905 microfilm reels.

498 magazines and newspapers.

65 phonograph records.

Besides the Old State Capitol, the Illinois State Historical Library and the Illinois State Historical Society operate two other **historic sites.** These are Clover Lawn, a handsome Victorian **mansion** in Bloomington, and the Carl Sandburg birthplace in

Galesburg. The historical society is also cooperating with the division of highways in placing historical markers at other historical sites in the state.

For those who cannot come to the historical sites, the society operates a **mobile** museum called the Robert R. McCormick Historymobile. Perhaps you have seen this historymobile when it visited your school or county fair.

The society aids the library in collecting all available material related to the history of Illinois. These include not only records of important events, but also other items that might not have seemed important at the time, such as personal letters and photographs. The Illinois State Historical Society also publishes a variety of materials for students and others interested in Illinois history.

Illinois State Museum

Unlike historical societies in some other states, such as Minnesota and Nebraska, the Illinois State Historical Society does not operate a state museum. It is under the Department of Registration and Education. The Illinois State Museum includes not only **exhibits** of the story of the people who have lived in the area, but also of the animals, plants and minerals of the state as well. Some general material on these subjects is also displayed in the museum.

The museum began in 1877 and was located in part of the present state capitol building. It moved across the street to a 50 by 60 foot room in the State

Dickson Mounds Museum.

Arsenal in 1903. Then in 1923 it moved to the fifth floor of the Centennial Building, which had been constructed on the state's hundredth birthday in 1918.

As time went on, more and more exhibits were added to the museum until it became quite crowded. At the same time the number of workers in the state offices which occupied the rest of the Centennial Building was also growing. Their working space had to be **shoehorned** into every available space. Some workers even had to walk though the state museum going to and from their offices. To relieve this crowding, the museum was moved to its present building in 1963.

133

A branch of the Illinois State Museum was opened at Dickson Mounds State Park in 1972. This park is the location of an Indian **burial mound.** Thus the Dickson Mounds Museum, which stands on top of the mound, tells the story of the life of the Indians of that region. One wing of the building contains an exhibit of the **excavation** of the Indian graves themselves.

Newspapers

Early settlers in Illinois had a difficult time keeping in touch with the outside world. Radio and television had not even been dreamed of then and there were no newspapers printed in the territory. Some news was brought by travelers coming up the rivers by boat or **overland** on foot or horseback.

This news would be many weeks or even months old, and not too **reliable.** The travelers might not have known all the details in the beginning and would have forgotten others during the trip. Some would also be inclined to stretch the truth a bit.

The settlers who could read had a more reliable source of information in letters and newspapers sent from back East. However, these, too, would be weeks or months old before they reached Illinois because of the slowness of transportation. The mails were also **infrequent.** Around 1810, even the larger towns received mail only twice a week.

Keeping up with the local news was a problem also. There undoubtedly was **gossip** then as there is

Traveling ministers, like the circuit rider shown here in this diorama, spread both religion and education in early Illinois.

now, but it was no more reliable than some of the tales told by travelers. For better information the settlers could check the trees and walls of buildings in their town. Often notices and news items were tacked up in these places for all to see. You have probably seen wanted posters displayed in this manner in western movies and TV shows.

This situation changed when Matthew Duncan established the first printing press in Illinois at Kaskaskia in 1814. With it Duncan began publishing the first newspaper in the territory, the "Illinois Herald," on September 6, 1814. Other newspapers followed. The "Shawnee Chief" was founded at Shawneetown on May 27, 1818.

These early papers could not, of course, do anything about bringing the news of the outside world to Illinois faster or more frequently, but they did provide a single place to find local news. They were published once a week and were only four pages long. Actually, they were a single sheet folded in half. These four pages contained mostly official publications such as new laws, advertisements and communications from local residents. For **national** and **international** news the papers had to depend on clippings from Eastern papers.

Then, as now, newspaper editors often championed **controversial,** and often unpopular, causes. One of these was Elijah Parish Lovejoy, a **crusading** abolitionist (antislavery) editor of the "St. Louis Observer," who fled across the river to Alton, seeking safety in a free state. However, most Illinoisans looked on **abolitionists** as a threat to the Union and so Lovejoy received a violent reception. As he came ashore, his press was dumped into the river.

This did not stop Lovejoy, who gathered some supporters and bought another press. With it he began publishing the "Alton Observer" in September 1836. The next year the state legislature **outlawed** abolitionist papers, and on the night of August 21 of that year a mob destroyed the press and the "Observer's" type. Lovejoy purchased new equipment with the help of Eastern backers, but the new press was dumped into the river soon after it arrived.

A mob attacks the warehouse where Lovejoy's press is stored, Nov. 7, 1837.

Finally a fourth press was delivered on November 7, 1837. It was stored in a large stone warehouse and defended by Lovejoy and his supporters. The next night a mob attacked and Lovejoy was shot to death, his friends driven off and the press destroyed.

This was not the end of the abolitionist **crusade**, however. It was now taken up by Benjamin Lundy, editor and publisher of the "Genius of Universal Emancipation" in Hennepin. Lundy, a farmer, died of overwork during the wheat harvest in 1839. The cause of antislavery was then taken up by the Lowell "Genius of Liberty," which was renamed the "Western Citizen" three years later and moved to Chicago.

A communications **revolution** began in Illinois with the delivery of the first telegram in 1848. Within two years many Illinois towns were linked by telegraph wires. Now newspapers could receive news of the outside world in days rather than weeks. Soon the service was improved to an instant **link** with the rest of the nation. In 1866, the first successful Atlantic cable was laid across the floor of the ocean. (Two earlier tries had failed.) Now Illinois was linked to Europe as well as to the United States. By this time practically every town in Illinois had at least one newspaper, and many had two **competing** papers. There were also some specialized papers. The first Negro newspaper, the "Conservator," was established in 1878.

Until the coming of radio and television, newspapers were the main source of information in Illinois. Whenever a news **bulletin** came in, the editor would call to the printers to "Stop the presses!" New type would then be set and the printers would run off a special edition called an extra. When there was more than one paper in a town, they would race to see who could be the first to get an extra on the streets.

When news was developing too fast to be printed up in an extra, the latest bulletins would be pasted on the windows of the newspaper office. Crowds would then gather on the sidewalk to read the latest news.

Radio and Television

Although the telegraph brought instant communications to the newspapers and to business, it did not bring it into the home. A person who wanted to

An early day radio.

send a telegram would have to go to the nearest telegraph station, where a **telegrapher** would **translate** his message into electric dots and dashes. When the reply came, the telegrapher would then have to translate it back into printed or spoken English.

This bottleneck was eliminated when the first telephones appeared in the 1870s. It was several more years before telephones came into general use, however. Voice broadcasting was not possible until 1900, and did not really come into use until 1919.

In the early twenties many Illinois citizens began listening to such pioneering stations as KDKA in Pittsburgh with homemade radios. These sets were powered by large batteries. Radios that plugged into the household current did not appear until the thirties.

At first there were no speakers for the early radios, so people had to listen with large earphones that resembled the earmuffs airport workers wear today for protection from jet noise. When two people wanted to listen to the same radio, they had to share the earphones.

These early radio listeners were often more interested in how many stations they could pick up, and from how far away, than in listening to the programs. Sometimes they would get impatient if the radio stations did not identify themselves often. Thus when the first radio station in Illinois, WDZ, began broadcasting from Tuscola in 1922, it was almost of more interest to listeners outside Illinois than to those in the state.

Broadcasting quality improved rapidly, and within ten years people became more interested in the programming than in the finding of stations. The number of stations also increased, and by the time World War II began many towns as well as large cities in Illinois had their own radio stations. The rural stations began by just broadcasting the **farm markets** at certain times of the day. Soon they added

An early day telephone.

music programs so that the farmers could locate the station before the market broadcast began. They also added other news and gradually extended their offerings to full broadcasting coverage.

Many stations in Illinois and across the nation also were linked together in **networks** so that the same program could be carried across the country. The first coast-to-coast hookup was made on February 8, 1924, and by 1927 there were two major networks in the United States. These networks broadcast not only music, but **comedy** and **drama** as well.

In the early 1930s Chicago was **dominant** in the production of network radio programs and later in television broadcasts. Many performers and newsmen got their starts in Chicago. Gradually, however, network programming production began to shift to Hollywood and New York in the late thirties.

Dramatic television programs actually got their start in Chicago. The first dramatic television program was broadcast over W9XAP in 1931. There were only a handful of television sets in the city to receive this **experimental** program. They had small circular screens and the picture they produced was black and white and not very clear—but it was a start. Regular television broadcasting did not come to Illinois until after World War II.

Today every person in Illinois has a choice of radio and television stations to listen to or to watch. How many stations are in your area, and which are your favorites?

Your local television and radio are the last link in a relay that brings news and entertainment to you from all over the world and even from far out in space. What do you think the early pioneers in Illinois would think of our modern communications systems?

Turn to the data section of this book and see how much information you can find about various kinds of communication systems in our state.

Chapter V
Transportation

Highways: Classes and Symbols

Look at your Illinois Highway Map. It is so full of lines that it almost resembles a spider's web, doesn't it? Do you know what all of these lines represent? If you said "roads," you are correct—but what kind of roads?

Look at the map **legend** and find the **symbols** that represent various types or kinds of roads. The major or more heavily traveled highways are of two types. These are called **Principal Through Highways** and **Other Through Highways.**

Another group of symbols indicates **Other Highways** which are those of secondary or lesser importance. These represent two-lane paved, oiled or graveled roads.

Principal Through Highways

These are the highways that carry the greatest amount of traffic. They include the major **interstate highways.** These are indicated in red, except for the **toll roads,** which are shown in yellow. Can you find these on your map?

Other Through Highways

These are indicated in black. We might call them **intermediate** highways. They are important roads, but they do not carry the heavy traffic of the principal through highways. Can you find examples of these on your map?

Other Highways

These are represented in blue. They are of secondary importance and carry the least amount of **traffic.** Can you find examples of these on your map?

Some highways are often referred to as **"trunk highways"** and others as **"arterial"** or **"feeder"** highways. What do you think these terms mean?

Let's take an imaginary trip from Springfield to Champaign. Look at your map and determine the best route to take. What kinds of highways will we travel on?

Can you find a town or city in Illinois that does not have a highway or road of **any** kind connecting it to the rest of the state?

Mileage Charts and Scale

There is a **mileage** chart in the lower left-hand corner of your map of Illinois. This lists thirty-six of the major cities in Illinois, four Illinois state parks and ten cities in neighboring states.

This chart tells you the mileage or distance between any two of the cities, or between any one of the cities and one of the state parks. When would this chart be helpful to a motorist?

Study the chart and find out how it works. How far is it from Cairo to Rockford? From Danville to Quincy?

Solve this problem: How long would it take you to drive from Aurora to Carbondale if you could maintain a speed of 50 miles per hour?

There is more mileage information contained on your map. Notice the tiny red numbers and red stars that appear next to highways. These are placed between towns and cities or highway **intersections** and show the distance between them. How far is it from Havana to Canton? From Nashville to Mount Vernon?

There are also small black numbers between towns and these also show distance. How far is it from Paris to Kansas?

There is still another method of measuring distance on your map. Look at the bottom of the legend of your map for the "Scale of Miles." In this case, your map will tell you that one inch on the map is equal to about twelve miles. Using your ruler, can you find out approximately how far it is from Decatur to Bloomington? From Alton to Edwardsville?

How many ways are there to find mileage distances on your map?

Early Transportation

Long before there were any man-made highways, Illinois was linked together by **natural** highways. These were the rivers, streams and lakes which extended out from the Mississippi River like branches on a tree. Along the banks of these watery roads were the **raw materials** for the boats the Indians used to travel on them.

Before the white settlers came, Illinois was nearly half forest. In the north, Indians peeled the bark

147

National Aeronautics and Space Administration

ERTS — 1 photograph of the Davenport, Iowa area. Can you find: Davenport, Moline and Rock Island (slightly left of center); Clinton, Iowa (upper center); Mississippi River (upper center to lower left); Muscatine, Iowa (left center) Illinois River (far right); Iowa River (lower left); Peoria (lower right); and Galesburg (lower center)?

from birch trees and fastened this to the frame of small tree branches to make a light, easily carried **canoe.** Farther south, where no birch trees grew, the Indians shaped their canoes out of logs. These were called dugout canoes.

With these canoes the Indians could travel almost anyplace in Illinois, and, in fact, in the Midwest. Sometimes the canoes had to be carried from one stream to another. This is called a **portage.**

When winter came, the lakes and rivers froze over, but the ice was seldom thick enough to make travel safe. So the Indians had to find other means of travel. Walking overland, they followed the buffalo trails, marking them with bent **saplings.** Some of these trees can still be seen today, now grown into elbow-shaped trees.

There were two main Indian trails. One was the Great Sauk trail from Rock Island to Lake Michigan, then north around the lake to Canada. The other was the St. Louis Trace from the falls of the Ohio (opposite the present site of Louisville) to Cahokia.

The Indians had no horses until after the white man came, so when they traveled overland they had to carry everything on their backs or put their dogs to work. For this they used a **travois,** a drag made of two crossed limbs fastened to the animal's back with straps of hide.

Whether on foot or in canoes, the Indians of Illinois evidently traveled far trading with other tribes. Archaeologists investigating the Indian graves at Cahokia have found **conch** shell beads from the Gulf of Mexico, rolls of Great Lakes copper, **mica** from the Carolinas, and **flint** arrowheads from their own Midwest.

Early keelboat used in fur trade.

Pioneer river boats at early day Moline.

Pioneer Transportation

The first French explorers used canoes, as did the Indians, but as the fur trade increased, larger boats were developed. The first step up from the canoe was the **pirogue** or dugout. This was a kind of super canoe forty or more feet long made from the trunk of a tree, usually a sycamore or a cottonwood. Next was the **bateau** (French for boat), which was a flat plank boat with pointed ends. When a plank was added along the bottom of such a craft, to make the steering easier, it became a **keelboat.**

The bateaus and keelboats could carry up to forty tons of **cargo** and a crew of three downriver and six coming upstream. One would steer with a long pole similar to those used by **gondoliers** in Venice, Italy. The reason a double-sized crew was needed on the upstream trip was that the boat could ride the current all the way down to New Orleans. On the return trip, however, the boat had to fight the current.

Besides rowing the boats, sails were also used and sometimes the men hauled the craft along with ropes from the shore.

Settlers followed the traders down the river into Illinois. They came floating down the river on a variety of boats. Besides the boats used by the traders, they used a variety of others. These included **skiffs** carrying 500 to 20,000 pounds, and **oblong** Kentucky boats ten to fourteen feet wide and twenty to fifty feet long, sided and roofed, and guided by huge oars.

151

Wagons on main street, Peru, Illinois, 1866.

The Kentucky boats were also called arks. This was quite an apt name as the boats carried three or four families, their furniture, farm equipment and livestock. These boats sold for around $75. When the settlers reached Illinois, they either sold their boats to others going farther downstream or used the wood in them to build cabins or to make fires.

The settlers who could not afford river transportation came overland by wagon, horseback or on foot. Some settlers chose to come overland rather than risk the storms on the Great Lakes.

As they followed the Indian trails, the hooves of their horses and oxen and the wheels of their heavy wagons widened the narrow trails into roads. The settlers and traders also made some new roads of their own.

Fur trader Gurdon Saltonstall Hubbard wanted to avoid the difficulties of the Chicago portage from the Chicago River to the La Salle River in 1818. He used ponies on a trail south from Chicago to the Wabash River. This was the only clearly marked route to Wabash County and it became known as Hubbard's **trace.** Later it became a state road and it is now part of State Street in Chicago.

Also in 1818, the first "highway" in the United States, the National Road, was finished from Cumberland, Maryland, to Wheeling, Ohio. It reached Vandalia in 1852.

This National Road was nothing like today's interstate highways. It was more like a long, narrow clearing through the woods. In approving a similar road from Shawneetown to Kaskaskia in 1820, Congress required that it be "cut thirty-three feet wide, with stumps to be very low."

Travel over such roads was naturally quite slow even for horse-drawn wagons. For example, the **memoir** of John Mason Peck tells of his trip to Illinois with his wife and three children in a wagon drawn by one horse. The journey began on July 25, 1817, at Litchfield, Connecticut. It says, "Nearly one month was occupied in passing from Philadelphia through the state of Pennsylvania over the Alle-

153

gheny Mountains, till on the 10th of September he passed into Ohio. Three weeks he journeyed in that state, and on the 23rd of October, recrossed the Ohio River into the state of Kentucky . . . and on the 6th of November, again crossed the Ohio River into the Territory of Illinois at Shawneetown."

As settlement increased in Illinois, the farms were soon producing enough supplies to send to market. Many businessmen and some farmers built flatboats to float their goods down the river to New Orleans. When they arrived two or three months later, they sold their goods for whatever they would bring and sold the boats for lumber. They then walked back to Illinois, running the danger of being robbed along the way.

Travel was more an adventure than a pleasure in Illinois also. There was danger from robbers, and the roads were muddy during the January **thaw** and when it rained. There were few **inns** and these were just large houses with two or three rooms for the guests to share.

The citizens of Illinois made a number of efforts to improve overland transportation. One of these was the **plank road,** a Russian invention which had been tried successfully in Canada. The Illinois State Legislature approved the building of these roads in 1847. By September of the next year a three-inch-thick road was laid from Chicago ten miles to Duffy's Tavern at Riverside. (In those days a tavern was

154

The Early "Corduroy Road."

another name for an inn.) This road cost $16,000 and was a toll road.

Other plank roads followed, and soon there was one leading **inland** from almost every steamboat landing on the river. However, these roads were not kept up and the planks rotted and warped. They were all abandoned before 1851. By this time a network of railroads was spreading across the state.

Trains became the main means of transportation and roads were neglected until the coming of the automobile around the turn of the century.

Not all the settlers who came to Illinois stayed. Some moved on when the state became too civilized for them. Others, not having found fortunes in Illinois, went further west to search for wealth.

One group was driven out of Illinois. These were the Mormons who had settled in Nauvoo. Their neighbors felt threatened by the numbers of Mormons and by their **religious beliefs.** On June 27, 1844, the Mormon leader Joseph Smith and his brother Hyrum Smith were arrested and taken to the nearby Carthage jail where they were slain by a mob.

All that summer fighting between the Mormons and other settlers increased until the Mormons' new leader, Brigham Young, determined to leave Illinois. That winter all of Nauvoo, including the Mormon temple, was turned into a wagon factory. The Mormons sold their land and homes to buy horses and supplies for their westward **trek.**

In February of 1845, the first group of Mormons crossed the river with Brigham Young, and a thousand a week followed. As one account of the times says, "Ferryboats were crowded and the riverbank lined with **fugitives,** sadly waiting their turn to pass over and take up their solitary march to the wilderness."

It was indeed a march. There were not enough horses or oxen to go around, and many Mormons had to pull their belongings across the prairie in handcarts.

Mormon Hand Carts.

Steamboats and Towboats

In 1811, Cairo saw the beginning of a new era of river transportation as the first steamboat, the "New Orleans," chugged by on her way down the Ohio and Mississippi rivers to the city for which she was named. Five years later a new **innovation** made it possible for steamboats to travel on even shallower rivers. This was the placing of the **boilers** on the first deck instead of deep in the **hold.** This meant that the bottoms of the boats were only two or three feet below the surface of the water. With this new advantage, steamboat traffic increased rapidly. By 1820, seventy boats were plying the rivers, and in 1828, 3,700 steamboats docked at Cairo.

The steamboats on the lower Mississippi and Ohio rivers became huge floating palaces two or three stories high and nearly a block long. They pro-

Early stern wheeler Steamboat.

vided their passengers with every **luxury** the nineteenth century could offer, including rich wood paneling and deep pile carpeting. Besides these passenger boats, there were boats of almost every other variety. Perhaps you have seen the musical "Showboat" which is set on one of these specialized boats.

The larger steamboats stopped at St. Louis, where their cargoes were transferred to smaller boats for the trip up the shallower and narrower upper Mississippi and Illinois rivers. The major destination of many of these steamboats was Galena, on the upper Mississippi, to literally get the lead out. The town Galena was named for the lead sulphite ore that was mined in the hills near there.

When steamboat travel was at its peak, every boy along the rivers dreamed of one day becoming a steamboat pilot just as perhaps you dream of becoming an airline pilot. The two jobs were quite similar. The boats had to avoid dangers in the river just as an airliner must avoid **hazards** in the sky. In flood times there were huge tree branches floating downstream, and when the water was low the boat could get stuck on a **sandbar.** On the upper Mississippi and Illinois rivers there were **rapids** which the boats had to pass.

Beginning in 1872, some of the hazards were eliminated along the Illinois River. **Dams** were built to raise the water over the rapids, and **locks** were made to carry the boats past the dams. A lock is a kind of

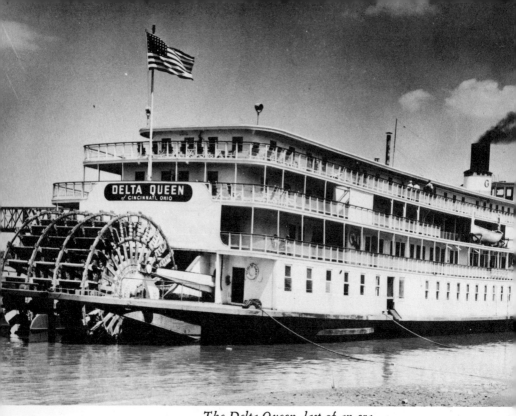

The Delta Queen, last of an era.

elevator for boats with huge doors both upstream and downstream. When a boat enters from downstream, water is pumped in to raise it to the level of the water behind the dam. When a boat comes downstream, the water is drained out of the lock, lowering the boat to the level of the water below the dam.

Steamboats came to the Great Lakes later than they came to the rivers. The first lake steamer did not reach Chicago until 1837. Several years before this the federal government had improved the Chicago **harbor.** The mouth of the Chicago River was widened eighty feet and dredged to eight feet deep.

By 1872, the age of steamboats was fading. Rail-

160

Chicago, A World Port

roads had taken over all their business. Today there is only one steamboat that makes regular stops at Illinois river towns, the "Delta Queen." There are a few other **miniature replicas** of the old steamboats operated for tourists.

The rivers are not deserted, however. Today towboats, at least as large as the smaller steamboats, push strings of up to fifty **barges** up and down stream. These barges carry a variety of often vital bulk cargoes such as coal, sand, gravel, iron, steel, petroleum products and chemicals.

While the steamboats could not operate during the winter, the towboats operate the year around. In winter the heavy barges break up the ice and push

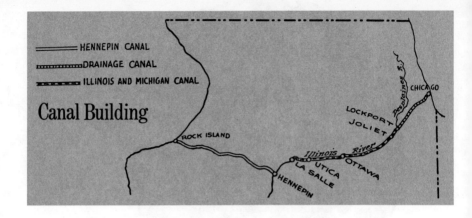

it aside. Only during high water are the towboats kept off the river, and then only so that their **wakes** will not damage the water-softened **levees.**

Waterways

The two great natural transportation routes of North America meet in Illinois. These routes are the branching **tributaries** of the Mississippi and the St. Lawrence-Great Lakes system. Today these systems are joined by a **canal,** but in the early days there was only a temporary, natural connection when the floodwaters of the Des Plaines and Chicago rivers mingled to form a muddy lake flowing in both directions. The rest of the year there was a portage of about four miles between the two rivers.

Many citizens of Illinois dreamed of making this temporary connection into a permanent canal through which steamboats could sail from the Illinois River to Lake Michigan. However, a year after the construction of the Illinois and Michigan Canal began on August 4, 1836, it was found that this deep canal would be too expensive. So, a smaller waterway using special canal boats was built. Even this took twelve years to build, and cost six and a half million dollars.

Let us take an imaginary trip to New Orleans from Chicago in 1848. We start our journey on the Illinois and Michigan Canal in July. This is just three months after the canal opened on April 23, 1848, but already seventy boats are moving up and down the canal. We are among ninety people riding the boat, which looks much like one of the old pioneer keelboats.

We have picked one of the luxury express craft, called a **packet boat,** so the team of horses pulling the boat with a long rope, trots along the tow path beside the canal at a brisk three and a half miles per hour. Along the way we pass slower moving boats whose teams plod along at only two and a half miles per hour. We also pass through seven locks and under twenty-five bridges on our ninety-six-mile journey from Chicago to La Salle.

At La Salle we will change to steamboats which have traveled as far up the river as they can. The trip from La Salle to New Orleans will take just one week. The return trip will take about a month because the steamboat must fight the current on the upstream trip. How did you like our imaginary trip?

EARLY
TRANSPORTATION ROUTES
TO CHICAGO

Like the steamboats, the Illinois and Michigan Canal lost business when the railroads came along, and it was abandoned in 1933. By this time, however, a new canal had been built. This was the Chicago Sanitary and Ship Canal. It came about as the result of a six-inch rainfall in the summer of 1885, which flushed the Chicago sewers into the Chicago River. The river emptied the **sewage** into Lake Michigan— the city's water supply.

Polluted drinking water had long been a problem in Chicago, but this brought matters to a head. The solution to this problem was to reverse the flow of the Chicago River. This was begun in 1889. A 28-mile-long canal was dug from the Chicago River to

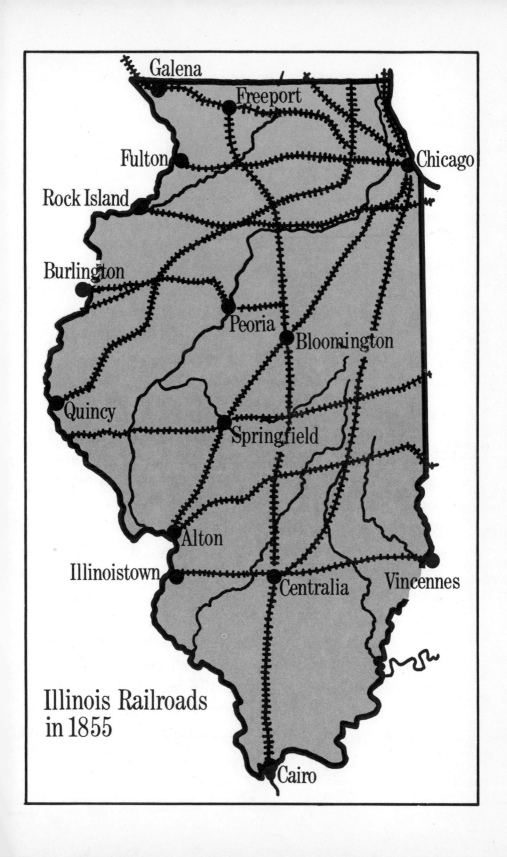

Illinois Railroads
in 1855

the Des Plaines at Lockport. Locks were placed at the mouth of the Chicago River (which was now its source) to control the flow of water.

On the back of your Illinois Highway Map there is a map of Chicago and vicinity. Can you find the Illinois and Michigan Canal and the Chicago Sanitary and Ship Canal on it?

The Chicago Sanitary and Ship Canal was dug deep enough for large boats and even small ships to travel. On March 5, 1953, the 634-foot "Marine Angel" reached Lake Michigan on a voyage from the Gulf of Mexico. She was the longest ship ever to pass through the canal. Thus the dream of the early citizens of Illinois became a reality.

Railroads

The first railroad in Illinois and, in fact, the first west of the Alleghenies, was a private road constructed in 1837. It ran from Illinoistown (now E. St. Louis) to coal mines in the **river bluffs** six miles away. The trains ran on strap iron rails nailed on wooden boards and spiked to ties laid directly on the ground. At first the trains were pulled by horses, and later wood-burning steam engines were brought in.

In January 1840, another railroad, the Northern Cross, was completed from Meredosia to Jacksonville. Two years later it reached Springfield. This railroad's name comes from the fact that it was part of a vast internal improvements scheme of the state legislature. There was also to be a Southern Cross

Illinois Central Gulf Railroad

Chicago, the foot of Madison Street and Michigan Avenue, 1864.

Railroad across the southern part of the state. These were part of a vast network of railroads, canals and roads that were to spread across Illinois. The scheme went **bankrupt** in 1841, leaving the state deep in debt. The only success of all the internal improvements was the Illinois and Michigan Canal.

Riding the Northern Cross was more hazardous than traveling the muddy roads. The strap iron rails had a tendency to curl up and stab the cars—and sometimes the passengers. Also the two iron horses, as the engines were nicknamed, had to stop often for more wood and water. These two engines, the "Rogers" and the "Illinois," soon broke down because of the lack of spare parts. After that, what little traffic remained was pulled by mules.

The Northern Cross was sold to a private company in 1847. This company laid new tracks and completed its line from Naples to Springfield on August 23, 1849. It is now part of the Norfolk and Western Railroad.

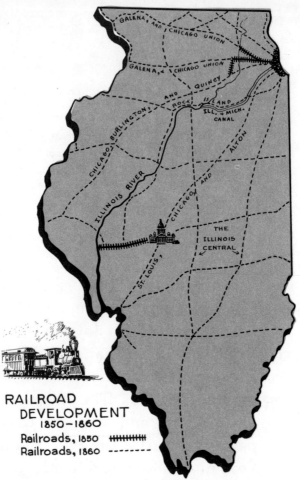

RAILROAD
DEVELOPMENT
1850–1860
Railroads, 1850 ┼┼┼┼┼┼┼┼
Railroads, 1860 --------

By 1848, a network of privately owned railroads was beginning to spread across the state. The first successful railroad in Illinois, the Galena and Chicago Union Railroad, was built by **financier** William B. Ogden. In 1848, a secondhand steam locomotive was delivered to Chicago by lake steamer and began operating on a six-mile stretch of strap iron track. The tracks were gradually extended westward to Galena.

Building railroads across Illinois.

This was the start of a railroad building boom in Illinois, and by 1855 the state had 2,005 miles of track—more than any other Western state. The Illinois Central line, which carried lead from Galena to Cairo, was the longest in the nation.

At first the Chicago merchants were afraid that the railroads might **bypass** their city. However, they need not have worried. Chicago is a natural **terminal** for the railroads, and, by 1857, eleven lines ran into the city. Chicago also began producing equipment for the railroads.

An Illinois man made it possible for people to be comfortable when they traveled on a train. His name was George Pullman, and he invented the sleeping car for trains in 1865. He became very rich and decided to build a town. He hired the best **town planners** and built a town just for his workers. It was called Pullman, and is now a part of Chicago.

As the railroads began to dominate transportation, they charged higher and higher rates. To **regu-**

Illinois Central Gulf Railroad

Illinois Central's tracks and yards on Chicago lakefront, 1865.

The Pioneer, early locomotive.

Illinois State Historical Library

Amtrak Intercity RR Passenger Service
Modern Amtrak locomotive.

Amtrak Intercity RR Passenger Service
Cab of an Amtrak Turboliner.

late the railroads, the Illinois Legislature in 1871 organized the Railroad and Warehouse Commission (now called the Illinois Commerce Commission). Sixteen years later the Federal Government also began regulating railroads when Congress created the Interstate Commerce Commission.

Today railroads have been losing business to planes, trucks and buses—especially in passenger service. To improve the passenger service, the Federal Government's Intercity Railroad Passenger Service, nicknamed Amtrack, took over the passenger trains on May 1, 1971. As part of this improvement Amtrack began operating fast, luxurious French **turbo trains** between Chicago and St. Louis regularly on October 15, 1973.

Automobiles

Except for the steamboats and railroads, everything in Illinois in the nineteenth century moved by muscle power, either human or animal. There were as many different types of horse-drawn or ox-drawn vehicles then as there are different kinds of motor vehicles today. They were, however, generally smaller than the motor-driven vehicles that now perform the same tasks.

Around the turn of the century, the first automobiles appeared in Illinois. These early cars were called "horseless carriages"—which is exactly what they were. Horses were frequently frightened into running away by the strange machines. It was not

Horse and carriage of the Amish people.

Early Ford motor cars.

Educational Affairs Dept., Ford Motor Co.

MODEL A
FIRST FORD MOTOR COMPANY CAR
1903

MODEL B TOURING CAR
FIRST FOUR-CYLINDER FORD
1905

MODEL K TOURING CAR
FIRST SIX-CYLINDER CAR
1906

MODEL T TOURING CAR
FIRST FORD MODEL T
1909

the sight of a carriage running by itself that frightened the horses so much as their chugging noise and frequent shotlike backfires.

The horseless carriages did not always stay horseless. They were subject to frequent breakdowns, and teams of strong horses were the only towing service available. Horses were also frequently called upon to pull cars which had become stuck in the muddy roads.

Naturally the automobile drivers began pushing for **paved roads.** However, the farmers were not interested in paying the costs for a city man's pleasure. A simple solution to this problem was found in 1911, when a state law was passed putting the money collected from auto license fees into road improvements.

The number of cars in Illinois increased rapidly and by 1918 there were 340,000 cars in the state. Already the police were having problems controlling speeders and cars with noisy **mufflers.** They were also warning the motorists to turn their lights on at night. Now the automobile was no longer a rich man's plaything. Practically everybody owned a car.

Now the state really began moving on road improvements. Aid was also received from Congress which approved **matching** state funds with federal money, and in 1918 Illinois passed a six-million-dollar bond issue. During Governor Len Small's term, from 1921 to 1929, Illinois highways became the envy of every other state.

Highway improvements are still continuing today. Do you think we need more and better roads? Or do you think the money would be better spent on some other form of transportation?

The Airplane

In 1896, Octave Chanute, a retired French-American civil engineer, and his assistant, A. M. Herring, set up an aeronautical research **laboratory** in Chicago. Two years earlier Chanute had a book on "Progress in Flying Machines" published. This book was the main source of information and guidance for the Wright brothers in their work to develop an airplane. The Wright brothers and other aviation pioneers also frequently got advice from Chanute as their experiments continued.

Besides writing about flying and consulting with aviation pioneers, Chanute did quite a bit of research on his own. He and his assistants built **gliders** which he test flew at the Indiana **dunes,** just around the bend of Lake Michigan from Chicago. In some three hundred flights Chanute and his assistants developed the **biplane** (two-winged) glider.

For the first twenty years the principles developed by Chanute guided the builders of airplanes, and these principles are still important today.

For many years after the Wright brothers made their first airplane flight in 1903, pilots were mainly

National Air Museum, Smithsonian Institution

Chanute Biplane glider, 1897.

An early 1920's Biplane.

National Aeronautics and Space Administration

One of first air mail planes.

occupied with exhibition flying. They also tried to see how far, fast, or high their **fragile** planes would go. One of these flights was made in 1910 to win a prize of $10,000 offered by H. H. Kohlsaat of the "Record-Herald" for a flight from Chicago to Springfield on the opening day of the state fair.

To win this prize, Walter R. Brookins, an employee of the Wright brothers, took off from Chicago before a crowd of 30,000. He made the trip to Springfield in seven hours and twenty minutes, stopping briefly at Mount Pulaski. Today airliners make the trip from Chicago to Springfield nonstop in about an hour.

Airlines got their start in Illinois with the beginning of airmail service between Chicago and New

York. Chicago soon became a center for airline travel just as it had for water, rail and highway traffic.

By 1931 there were eight airline companies flying to and from Chicago. Their routes covered 5,072 miles and reached cities as far away as New York, San Francisco and New Orleans. The first regular overseas flight began in Illinois on November 19, 1945, when American Airlines started weekly service between Chicago and London.

By this time Chicago Midway Airport, dedicated in 1929, had become the world's busiest airport and was overcrowded. So O'Hare Airport was opened in 1946. Soon all the airlines moved to this new airport, which was ten times as large as Midway. For a time Midway was closed until about 1968, when O'Hare, now the world's busiest airport, became overcrowded. Some airlines then began moving back to Midway.

Today twenty-seven airlines fly to and from Chicago's airports. Airline service in the rest of the state, however, is dominated by Ozark Airlines, which began service in 1950. Besides Ozark there are only a few **commuter** airlines. These airlines fly small planes usually carrying about eighteen passengers. A forty-eight passenger plane for them is as large as a **jumbo jet** is for a major airline. Some of these commuter airlines fly into Meigs Field, an airport serving small planes on Lake Michigan in downtown Chicago.

Chicago Convention and Tourism Bureau

Chicago's O'Hare International Airport, the world's busiest.

Part of the jet fleet of Ozark Airlines.

Ozark Airlines

Besides the three airports in Chicago, there are many other airports in Illinois. Your Illinois Highway Map will show you where these airports are located. Which airports are closest to you? Which of these has scheduled air service and which does not? Turn to the data section of the book and see how much information you can find about transportation in Illinois.

Chapter VI

Agriculture and Industry

Natural Resources

The land and water of Illinois have provided a rich variety of **resources** without which agriculture and industry could not have prospered as they have over the years. Some states have been blessed with mineral deposits such as gold, silver or copper. (Can you name them?) Others have their rich iron ore deposits. (Can you name some of these states?) The land of Illinois offered a different kind of gold. The yellow grains, wheat and corn, have been gold for Illinois. These "golden" products have provided the **foundation** on which a good share of the state's industrial growth has been made. "Black gold," oil and coal, have also been discovered in the state and can be classified as other resources to be given up by the land.

Other resources that the earth has released for important use in the state are: sand and gravel; stone, such as sandstone, limestone, dolomite, lead, fluorspar, and several types of clay. Many of these mineral resources are not being mined in any great amount at present, but exist in quantities great enough to rate as important products for the future.

Growth of Industry

Industry flourished in Illinois from the time of early pioneers until the present time. The fur traders were the forerunners of industry. They were followed by **gristmills** and transportation enterprises. Businesses were started, providing goods and ser-

Freeport Journal-Standard

Illinois Dairy Cattle.

Illinois farms use modern machinery.

vices for the people engaged in these industries. Agricultural crop production soon took over the main place in Illinois industry, replacing the fur trade in importance. Illinois became one of the leading agricultural states in both crop and animal production, although today the state's income is produced in great part by nonagricultural sources.

Food processing is a leading industry today, and the state is a leader in such product areas as dairy and meat products and livestock feed.

Oil was discovered in parts of Illinois, and this industry has contributed much to the industrial importance of the state, providing petroleum products as well as natural gas.

Railroads and modern highways have crisscrossed the state, linking the United States from coast to coast, and in this way transportation might be considered a major industry also.

These industries grew over the years, creating more jobs and the demand for more people. The ears of the world were listening, and people came from all over the world to settle in Illinois.

Growth of Manufacturing

Manufacturing or the creating of **man-made** or **man-changed** products for market has grown steadily over the years, and at present Illinois ranks as a leading manufacturing state.

Small gristmills (for grinding grain into flour and meal) sprang up across the state in the early days, taking advantage of the abundance of water available for power.

Other kinds of manufacturing followed the early gristmills, such as pottery factories, furniture factories, **foundries,** machine shops, breweries and meat and dairy product processing operations. These manufacturing concerns provided materials for a growing state as well as providing products much in demand from other states and from countries around the world.

In more recent years the state has continued to increase its number and kinds of manufacturing operations, and has become a leader in the following areas: food processing, machine and tool production, printing and publishing, insurance, electrical products, farm machinery, irrigation equipment, metal buildings, mobile homes, automotive parts and communication equipment.

Manufacturing, from the early mills to the elaborate plants of today, has made Illinois a manufacturing market center for the world.

The Pioneer Farmers

The first settlers to break the prairie sod and grow crops found the rich soil much to their liking. They decided to stay, and sent word to their friends and relatives in distant places, telling about their "new land."

Tales of the great **potential** of the vast unbroken prairie and of land available, free for the taking,

186

An early day steam threshing rig.

spread far and wide, and soon people began to come into the area in search of their fortunes. At first, only small numbers came to brave the **wilderness hardships,** but soon wave after wave of **immigrants** arrived, searching for their "promised land" or new life. Crops were planted, towns and settlements came into being, and roads were built, linking communities to the outside world. The wilderness was soon conquered by the adventurous people of the frontier.

These early farms were small compared to the farms of today, for all work had to be done by hand, or with the limited help of horses or oxen. Machinery was almost unheard of, and what little there was usually was hand made on the farm. Farm homes were often miles apart and many miles from the nearest town or settlement.

Early Trials, Tribulations and Social Life

Illness was common to early pioneer homes. **Epidemics** of measles, mumps, scarlet fever, typhoid, diphtheria, influenza, and sometimes smallpox, took their toll. Tuberculosis was also common, and sometimes cholera found its way to the area, carried up the Mississippi by steamboat travelers from the South. Medical treatment was limited and **crude.** The few horse and buggy doctors had very little in the way of medicines, and even their meager supplies were only slightly effective. In sickness and in childbirth, neighbor helped neighbor, since doctors were usually too far away to be called on. Newspapers of the day carried scores of ads for **patent medicines.** These were called "**antibilious, cathartic,** vegetable and **ague** pills," and there were great varieties of syrups, **bitters, pitch, liniment,** pain extractors, Indian cures, and **balms.** The two most important books in the pioneer home were the Bible and the **doctor book,** and both were read often and carefully.

The early settlers faced many other hardships. There were winter blizzards, summer prairie fires, and hungry hordes of grasshoppers.

The settlers survived all these hardships, however, and learned to satisfy their needs by making soap and candles, churning butter and weaving blankets and clothing. Clothing had to be mended often

Grasshoppers . . . they often ate every green plant in entire field.

Prairie fires were an early day threat.

Threats of hail and tornadoes caused early day farmers much concern. Do they yet today?

Early day farms were often snowbound.

to prolong its life, and often the busy mother had to work alongside her husband in the fields. Children were not idle, and seldom had time to get bored or into mischief, for they were expected to work in the fields at a very early age.

Life was hard on the frontier, but it had its pleasant side, too. Families were bound together by love, work and sharing, and communities or settlements were bound together in both work and social activities. Perhaps your parents or grandparents can recall more information about the following activities.

Grandma's Lye Soap

Early settlers had little choice in brands of laundry soap available in their day. In fact, their only choice was to make it themselves.

After **butchering** a hog, all of the fat was carefully trimmed and saved. This was placed in a huge black-iron kettle under which a hot fire was kept burning. Cans of **lye** were added and the mixture cooked and stirred until the proper **texture** was obtained.

Residue was ladled off the top and the remaining thick, white mixture was poured or **ladled** into wooden forms. When it hardened it provided bars of soap that would supply laundry needs for quite some time.

In using this soap, the housewife would scrape thin shavings from the bar into hot wash water, and as it dissolved it left a sort of sudsy water in which the family clothing was washed. It was harsh and hard on clothing, but it did clean fairly well and so accomplished its purpose. It was harsh on skin, too, as many youngsters of the time could verify through varied degrees of chapped skin.

The **rinds** or pork "cracklings" remaining after the fat was cooked from them were considered a **delicacy** by many youngsters, especially when eaten warm, and it is quite possible that a good many pioneer children went to bed with "crackling" good stomachaches when they ate too much.

Butchering Day

The early pioneers set up their own "do-it-yourself" meat markets, usually in the fall, in order to store up a supply of meat to last through the long winter months.

These "do-it-yourself" occasions usually had two or more families working together. This provided more hands for the job and enabled them to butcher several animals (usually hogs) in less time than if they worked individually.

First, the animals were killed and bled, then strung up on a makeshift **hoist** from which they were "scalded" or lowered into a barrel of boiling hot water. This process helped in scraping the hair from the skin of the animal.

The next process involved cutting the **carcass** into quarters and cutting the meat into the desired cuts. Tenderloin cuts were put on the cookstove soon after they were cut, and by evening the entire group sat down to one of the most delicious meals imaginable.

Much of the meat was ground and seasoned for sausage, which was stuffed into the cleaned intestine casings of the animal. The hams or shoulders were later hung in a **"smokehouse"** where they were heavily salted and smoked over a hickory fire. This **preserved** the meat and added a taste quality that would appeal to all appetites.

Nearly every part of the animal was used and very little went to waste. Fresh liver, tongue and "head cheese" were considered delicacies and, of course, "pickled pig's feet" became an item of considerable importance.

Husking and Quilting Bees

In the days of the early settlers, everyone helped each other when the need arose. They had to or they couldn't have survived.

This trait is still evident in our state today, but to a lesser degree than in the early days. Whenever there was a death in a family or the man of the house was ill, injured or away to war, neighbors would all gather at that particular farm on a designated day, bringing their own horses and wagons, and proceed to **"husk"** the entire field of corn in one day.

The women would usually go along on this special occasion and cook up quantities of food to feed the workers. Often each woman would bring along some item of food, and by **pooling** their resources, would prepare a meal equal to the finest **smorgasbord** ever seen.

During the day, when not busy preparing food, the women would work at what was known as a **"quilting bee."** The purpose of this was to make a quilt or comforter for adding to the family's bedding supply. A wooden frame was set up and two cloths placed around some **"batting"** and stretched across the frame. The edges were then sewn and each woman would attach a square (about 12 by 12) consisting of decorative and colorful needlework.

When all of these sections were sewn to the cloth, it resulted in a beautiful and useful article of bedding.

Each lady would **embroider** her name or initials onto her section, and sometimes there might have been a little unspoken **competition** among them to see whose work stood out above all the rest.

The family receiving the help on these special occasions was usually not embarrassed nor their **pride** damaged, for they knew they would be helping someone else at some other time in just the same way.

The Box Social

One of the early day social events of the year was the box social.

This was an event usually held in February, close to Valentine's Day, perhaps because of the romantic influence of Cupid at that particular time. The event was usually held at the one-room school in the area, and a special program planned for the evening would include plays, skits, readings and special music renditions.

Each of the fairer sex, from teen-ager on up, would bring a beautifully decorated box containing fried chicken, cake or cookies and other taste tempters. These boxes were to be assembled in **secrecy** so that no one knew to whom they belonged.

After the program, an **auctioneer** would sell each box to the highest bidder, the money usually going to some community or **charitable** cause. Many young men tried to get advance knowledge of what a certain young lady's valentine box would look like, and in some instances the young ladies would provide a **clue** to guide the **bidding** of someone they favored.

One can imagine the excitement on occasion when two or more young men ended up trying to outbid each other for a particular box.

All boxes had to be sold, and when the bidding was over, the man would step forward, pay for the box, and then the owner of the box would be identified and the two would then sit together and eat the contents, while either enjoying or enduring the other's company for the balance of the evening.

Sometimes a few of the older men would take great delight in making a certain young man pay dearly for a certain box by staying in the bidding

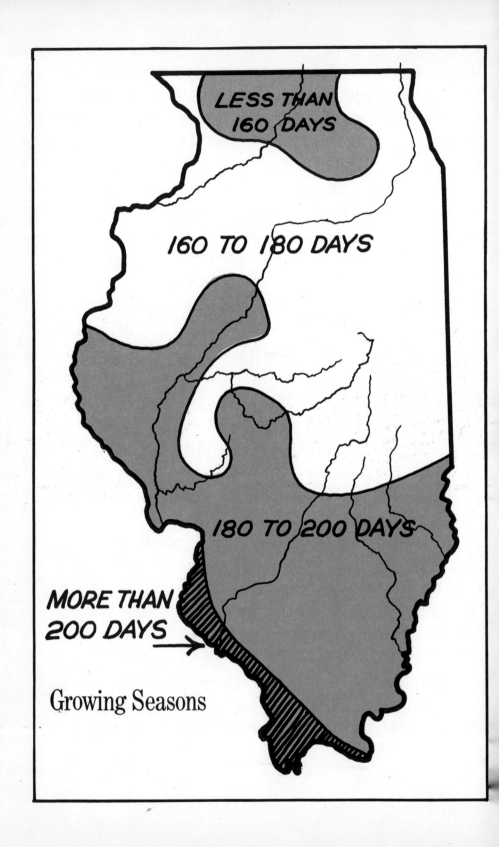

LESS THAN 160 DAYS

160 TO 180 DAYS

180 TO 200 DAYS

MORE THAN 200 DAYS →

Growing Seasons

for quite some time. This probably caused some wife to question whether or not her husband was doing it just for the fun of watching the young man squirm or whether he might really have wanted to buy the young lady's box. All of this added to the occasion, however, and there was always that long ride home in which to discuss the matter in greater detail.

Agriculture Over the Years

The Illinois State Agricultural Society, organized in 1853, helped farmers through its publications and by **sponsoring** the state fair. The state fair encouraged county fairs where farm products of all kinds were displayed in competition for the "biggest and best" prizes.

The growth of states west of the Mississippi River after the Civil War made competition for Illinois farmers. Do you think this competition was good or bad? Can you think of any reasons for your choice? Farmer organizations, called **granges,** were organized in 1868 to provide the farmers with a voice in **protesting** against economic conditions that found the railroads and warehouses taking most of their profit through high costs of shipping and storing.

In the 1920s, farm prices were so low and money so hard to obtain that many farms were lost through **mortgage foreclosures.** Other factors, such as **drouth** and soil **erosion,** also caused severe hardships for Illinois farmers. In the 1930s, government programs

197

Freeport Journal-Standard, Photos by Norman Templin
These happy girls won ribbons with their cattle at the County Fair.

A County Fair Champion and its proud owners.

Freeport Journal-Standard, Photos by Norman Templin

Mechanical corn picker enables today's farmer to grow and harvest more corn faster.

This photo shows contour stripcropping.

USDA Soil Conservation Service

were started that helped the farmers get back on their feet. These included such things as **government loans, soil conservation programs, contour plowing,** and **reforestation.** By the 1950s, Illinois farmers had again reached a high level of production and **prosperity.** Illinois farms made great progress through three major changes. The first was **mechanization.** New farm machinery was developed and made available to farmers that enabled them to farm more land in less time than before.

The second change was through **specialization.** Since the farmer no longer needed to be **self-sufficient,** he could specialize in one or more areas. Some specialized in corn and hog production. Others decided to raise beef cattle and grow the crops necessary to feed them on the farm. Others decided to raise dairy cattle or poultry along with crops they could sell each season. These are called **"cash crops."**

The third change was in the area of **experimentation.** By using new ideas such as **crop rotation,** contour farming, and later on adding nitrogen **fertilizers** to their soil, they found that they could raise better crops and increase the **yield** of these crops. Many farms began to operate on a **mass production** basis just as the big factories of industry were doing. Some farmers began feed lot operations, where they fed a large number of livestock a balanced diet of grain and feed, and then marketed the entire number at a preplanned time. When one such group of animals

Hybrid corn in Illinois.

was sold, another would be acquired, and the whole operation started over again.

Between 1850 and 1856, Illinois built over 2,100 miles of railroad track. This opened new markets to the farmers. Their products could be shipped to Chicago and from there, by both rail and water, to the East Coast and to Europe. With this new marketing system the farms of Illinois became more and more prosperous, and soon Illinois led the nation in agricultural production.

Today Illinois farms are far different from the farms of the early days. Thousands of miles of **all-weather roads** connect all the farms and cities of the state, and most farms today have modern homes with all of the luxuries and conveniences to be found anywhere.

201

Harvesting the hay (Alfalfa).

Today, only about one person in every five works on a farm, but farming is still important to Illinois. Illinois ranks third in agriculture among all the states. About 85 percent of Illinois is farmland. Some important crops in Illinois are corn, soybeans and wheat. Other important crops are cotton, fruits, vegetables and horseradish. The farmers also raise many cattle and hogs. Most of Illinois' corn is fed to the livestock, which in turn makes meat packing and processing an important related agriculture-based industry.

The Illinois Department of Agriculture provides farmers with crop and market information, feed and livestock inspection services and conservation information. Disease control programs for both crops and animals are provided as other helpful aids to the farmer. The related farm occupations, called **"agri-**

Illinois Central Gulf Railroad

A freight diesel pulls a train of covered hopper cars used to transport grain.

This new "snap on top" makes it possible to convert open topped coal carry-ing cars to covered grain carrying hopper cars.

Illinois Central Gulf Railroad

business," which provide thousands of jobs for Illinoisans in food packing and processing, shipping, and in the manufacture of farm machinery, are keeping agriculture the main part of the state's economy.

Contributions to Agriculture

Many people have made important **contributions** to Illinois agriculture. Let's look at a few of them. Perhaps you have heard their names before.

Hybrid seed corn was developed in Illinois. Lester Pfister, Gene Funk and C. L. Gunn were three developers. Because of their work, it was possible to grow more corn on the same fields.

Meat packing was also a big business in Illinois. The livestock was shipped to Chicago, where it was prepared for the **supermarket.** Some of the meat packers in Chicago were named Gustavus Swift, Philip Armour, Thomas Wilson, the Cudahys and Oscar Mayer. Do you recognize these names?

Other important Illinois inventors were Joseph Glidden of De Kalb, who invented **barbed wire,** and Gail Borden, who developed **condensed** milk in Elgin, in 1870.

The early settlers had trouble in their fields. They all used **plows** they had brought with them from the East. These plows were designed for the sandy soil of the East and didn't work well in the prairie soil. The dirt kept sticking to the plow, and the farmer had to stop every few steps to clean it.

A **blacksmith** named John Deere had just come

Illinois State Historical Library

Watching John Deere's miracle plow at work.

The first Deere Plow, 1838.

Deere and Company

McCormick's grain harvester invention (reaper).

from Vermont to settle in Grand Detour. As soon as he opened his **blacksmith shop,** he started to work on making a better plow. He used an old saw blade that had been used to cut up logs. He shaped the blade into a plow and at last the black dirt fell away and didn't stick to his plow. The year was 1838. This was very important because more land could be plowed for farming.

John Deere moved to Moline in 1847 to take advantage of the waterpower and transportation of the Mississippi River. By 1850, he was making 1,600 of his "singing plows" a year. Today Deere and Company is the oldest major manufacturing business in Illinois and the largest producer of **farm implements** in the world.

The farmers had help from another inventor, too. His name was Cyrus Hall McCormick. Mr. McCormick invented a **"reaper"** in 1834. This machine **harvested** the grain in the fields. Previously the farmer always had to cut the grain by hand. The McCormick plant was located in Chicago, and the whole plant burned during the Chicago fire. Another interesting thing is that a man in Rockford had also invented a reaper. McCormick thought that John H. Manny had stolen his idea. Manny hired a good lawyer named Abraham Lincoln, and he won the case.

The data section of your book contains a great deal more information about Illinois agriculture. Turn to that section and see how much additional information you can find.

Industry

Illinois, in addition to being one of the leading agricultural states, is also a leader in the area of **industry** and **manufacturing.** Nearly three fourths of the state's manufacturing plants are located in Cook County, but other cities such as Rockford, Peoria, East St. Louis, Decatur, Rock Island, Moline, Chicago Heights, Granite City, and Joliet are rapidly becoming **industrial centers** in their own right. Nearly everything you might imagine is manufactured in Illinois.

Think of any product in the following areas and it is quite likely that it is manufactured in Illinois: meat products, grain products, clothing, leather

The age of steel and welding in Illinois industry.

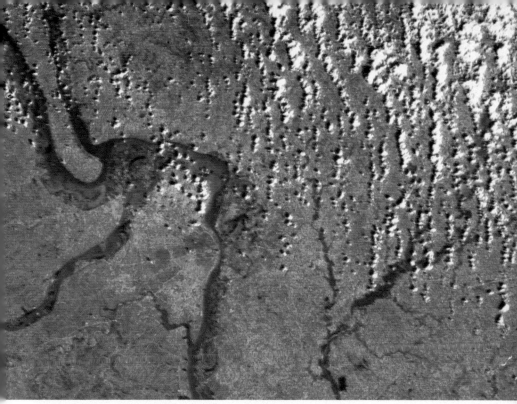

Nasa's Earth Resources Technology Satellite shows flooding along the Illinois, Missouri and Mississippi Rivers. Top photo in October 1972, bottom photo in March, 1973.

National Aeronautics and Space Administration

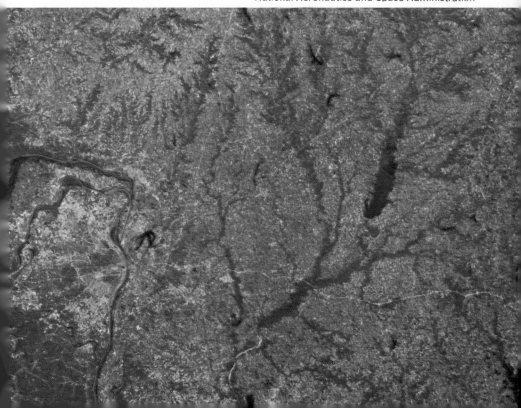

Farm scene in Galena area
Ill. Dept. of Business and Economic Development, Div. of Tourism

Fox River canoe scene
Ill. Dept. of Business and Economic Development, Div. of Tourism

Southern Illinois Farm scene
Ill. Dept. of Business and Economic Development, Div. of Tourism

Sailing on Rend Lake
Ill. Dept. of Business and Economic Development, Div. of Tourism

Camel Rock, Shawnee National Forest

Ill. Dept. of Business and Economic Development, Div. of Tourism

World's Largest Beverage Distillery, Peoria

Springer-Burkland, Peoria

Aerial view of Caterpillar Tractor Company

Caterpillar Tractor Company

Chicago at night

Ill. Dept. of Business and Economic Development, Div. of Tourism

What is this large
"grasshopper-like"
machine doing?

Big Muddy Wildlife Area, Turkey Bayou

Autumn foliage in Illinois

Galena in 1856.

goods, electrical products, farm machinery, petroleum products, wood products, industrial machinery, glass and paper containers, and transportation equipment. Perhaps you can add other items to this list that represent products manufactured or processed in the industries of the state.

Probably the first industry in Illinois was salt mining. The Indians had mined salt from the springs by Shawneetown in southern Illinois. The early settlers mined salt there, too. Today, cheaper sources of salt have been found, and salt mining is no longer the important industry that it was in early times.

Galena became an important early settlement in Illinois because lead was found there. Galena had the first post office in northern Illinois in 1826. The town grew rapidly because many men came from the East to try to find lead ore, just as the gold miners who went out West later on tried to find gold. Very little lead is mined in Galena anymore.

Illinois depends on many foundries and smelting and refining plants.

Illinois was and is an important manufacturer of wood products. Most of the lumber used to make the wood products is shipped down the Mississippi River from the forests of the northern states and Canada.

The steel industry is much the same. The iron ore and **taconite** come mostly from Minnesota, and the coal to fire the **furnaces** comes from Pennsylvania and Illinois, too, but the final product, steel, is made in Illinois. Many products are made from the steel manufactured in Illinois. Perhaps you have something made of steel manufactured in your town.

The manufacture of glass is very important in Alton and Streator, in the Owens-Illinois plants. They are large producers of bottles and other glass products.

Rockford was the home of the first automatic **hosiery** manufacturing plant.

Corn products, such as starch and oil, are important products made in Summit and Argo.

Peoria is famous for two products, Caterpillar tractors and whiskey, although today many other products are also manufactured there.

Wallpaper is manufactured in Joliet. Does your town manufacture some important product?

Mining in Illinois

Besides the salt and lead mentioned before, Illinois has other important mining. Coal and petroleum (oil) are the most important. The coal is mined either below the ground or by **strip mining,** which is done with big earth movers on the ground level. There is mining done in at least 29 counties. Do you live near a coal mine? It is said that Illinois has enough coal to supply the world for 130 years. Do you think this is a long time?

Coal is more important than lead in today's energy-hungry world. Layers of coal, some of it as much as fifteen feet thick, lie under two thirds of Illinois. The first barge of coal was shipped down the river from the state in 1810. The early mines **bored** straight into hills, then in 1842 the first **shaft** mine was dug down into the Illinois prairie.

Today the deepest shaft coal mine in the world is Peabody Mine Number 10 in Sangamon County. However, most of Illinois' coal is near the surface,

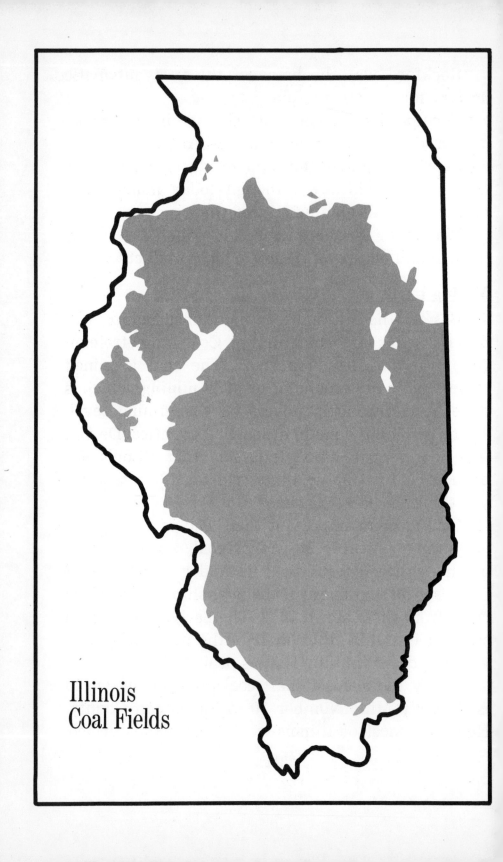

Illinois
Coal Fields

The Cherry Mine Disaster. Can you find out more about it?

so 56 percent of this state's coal comes from strip mines. Here huge shovels tear away the soil and upper layers of rock to get at the coal. Under Illinois law, when the miners are through, the land must be put back the way it was. In the meantime, not only land, but people and even towns have been uprooted by the shovels.

There is another problem. Although Illinois has enough coal to fuel the nation for the next hundred years, this coal is full of sulphur. When the coal is burned, the sulphur turns into poisonous **sulphur dioxide**—in other words, air pollution. Many scientists and engineers are now working on ways of getting the sulphur out of Illinois' coal. If they succeed, Illinois will not only have clean-burning coal, but another useful mineral product as well—sulphur.

The first discovery of coal in North America was made by Marquette and Joliet, who found what they called "Carbon de terre" in 1673. John Law, a Scottish promoter working for the French government, tried to encourage lead mining in the Fever River (now called the Galena River) district of northern Illinois in 1717. But little if any mining was done until the United States government took over the mines in 1802.

A **boom town** called Galena, for the lead ore, grew up soon after the first mining **lease** was granted early in 1822. A year later **smelting** began and 210 tons of lead were shipped down the river. By 1845, the output of lead had reached 2,700 tons—80 percent of the lead produced in the United States.

Three years earlier lead was discovered in Hardin County, on the Ohio River, in southern Illinois. When the lead mines in the Galena area began to run out in the 1860s, the Hardin County area became the state's major lead mining area. After 1900, the lead was produced jointly with **fluorspar,** which is used for **hydrofluoric acid** and coloring. One third of the fluorspar mined in the United States comes from Illinois, making this state the leader of the nation in the production of this mineral. World War II increased the demand for Hardin County's lead, and the output continued to grow, reaching a peak of 4,544 tons in 1955.

Fluorspar is an important product today in Hardin and Pope counties.

Deposits of limestone and dolomite are found in sixty counties, but the three leading counties are Cook, St. Clair, and Kankakee. Clay and clay products are important to twenty-five counties. Plants in these counties make stoneware, pottery, drain pipe, and bricks of all kinds.

Cement, sand and gravel are found in large quantities in La Salle, Lee, Massac, Ogle, Will and McHenry counties.

You can see that both mining and manufacturing are very important to all the people in Illinois and throughout the world.

Oil and Natural Gas

The first oil wells were drilled around the years 1883 to 1886, and by the year 1906, Illinois ranked third among the oil-producing states. Since that time, other states west of the Mississippi have become leading oil-producing states, but Illinois still remains the leading oil state east of the Mississippi. Today there are about 27,000 wells in the state producing nearly 50 million barrels of **crude oil** each year. About 41 counties in the state have oil wells. Does your county have oil wells? **Natural gas** is obtained from these oil fields, too, and this product is being used more and more in industry because it does not produce as much pollution as other fuels.

This "grasshopper-like" pump pulls oil from the depths of Illinois' rich earth.

New Sources of Energy

The **energy crisis** of the 1970s is causing planners to look beyond the existing **reserves** of **fossil fuels** (coal and oil) to the future when we will need new sources of energy to supply the power for our industries. Many forms of **nuclear** power are already in use. In Illinois, the world's first commercial nuclear power plant is located at Dresden, on the Illinois River. Argonne National Laboratory and the Atomic Energy Commission Accelerator are under construction at Weston, and will add to the energy output of the state. The world's first atom smasher is being

216

Commonwealth Edison Company

Zion Nuclear Power Station, 50 miles north of Chicago.

Dresden Nuclear Power Station, 50 miles southwest of Chicago. It began operation in 1960, the nation's first of its kind.

Commonwealth Edison Company

Synthetic Natural Gas (SNG) Plant, typical of those being built in Illinois for future fuel needs.

Control room of a typical electric generating station. What do you suppose the dials and gauges show?

built near Chicago, and it is estimated that Commonwealth Edison is getting more than a third of its supply from atomic power. Can you think of other sources that may provide energy in the future?

Protecting the Environment

Illinois has adopted rules and **regulations** to protect the **environment,** and to control the strip mining operations in the state. Any person or firm wishing to do strip mining must get a **permit** from the Department of Mines and Minerals. This permit will not be given unless those doing the mining will agree to **restore** the land surface to near natural condition. This means that the land will have to be leveled and topsoil spread over the surface so that **vegetation** can once again grow there. All **toxic** materials left from the mining operation have to be covered with soil to prevent the acid content from polluting lakes and streams. This protection and preservation of the environment is important to the people of the state today. What do you think people living in Illinois in the year 2000 will think of our environmental protection laws of the 1970s?

Science and Invention

There have been great scientific discoveries in Illinois, too, that have changed the world. Probably the most important event took place in Chicago on December 2, 1942. This was the control of the **atom.** It was the first **nuclear chain reaction** by controlled **fission** of uranium **isotope** U-235.

An Italian scientist, Enrico Fermi, was put in charge of a secret project at the University of Chicago. He and his fellow scientists made a huge pile from layers of uranium and graphite. Just 42 people were on hand to watch the cadmium-plated rod withdrawn from the experimental atomic pile. Mr. Fermi won the Nobel Prize for **unleashing** the controlled energy of the atom.

Mrs. Fermi was giving a party that night for some of their scientist friends. She knew nothing about her husband's secret work and couldn't understand why everyone was congratulating him. Few realized at that time that the experiment would lead to the building of the **atomic bomb** by the United States and the opening of the **Nuclear Age.**

The first Nobel winner from America was a physics professor at the University of Chicago. Albert A. Michelson won the prize for his development of the **Interferometer** and other **precision** tools for measuring the properties of light.

The first practical **wire recorder** was invented in Chicago in 1939. Marvin Camras then developed the modern **magnetic tape recorder** in 1945.

There have been other inventions made in Illinois, but the creations of Deere, McCormick, Michelson, Camras and Fermi did the most to change the way of life of people all over the world.

Chapter VII
Recreation

Who shall I say caught the fish, Grandpa?

Outdoor Recreation in Illinois

The "Land of Lincoln" offers sport and **recreation** for people all over the state. In the spring and summer, the lakes and streams provide the setting for fishing, boating, swimming and water-skiing. The many forest areas and conservation areas offer campers a **retreat** from busy daily **routine** and a chance to appreciate the wonders of nature much as the early **voyageurs** viewed it.

Tourism has become a major part of the state's **economy.** People from many other states travel about Illinois, visiting the many historical sites and enjoying the many camping and recreational facilities.

Winter also provides recreational activity. Ice skating, skiing and snowmobiling are popular with many Illinoisans.

In the fall, when the trees are arrayed in their brilliant colors, hunting is a major sport. Ducks, geese and pheasants have long been favorite targets of Illinois hunters, and the cornfields of the state offer some of the best pheasant hunting in the Midwest. Some forms of wild game have become smaller in number over the years due to the growing number of hunters, the clearing of forest lands and the draining of swamp areas. The Department of Conservation is concerned with protecting many kinds of wildlife from **extinction.** Some people predict that by the year 2000 some species of wildlife will no longer be

What season of the year is it?

Winter can be fun too!

Are there any Ski areas in Illinois?

with us due to hunting pressure and destruction of **natural habitat.** How can we save these forms of wildlife from becoming extinct?

Special Land Use

Much of Illinois' land area has been designated by the state and federal governments to serve special purposes. Illinois has 91 state parks and conservation areas, 64 camping areas, 4 state forests and 1 national forest area. In the past few years the state has acquired nearly 60,000 acres of recreational land, to be developed for present and future enjoyment. At a time when land is becoming scarce, Illinois has launched a land **acquisition** and **development** program to meet the growing needs of the people. This newly acquired land includes native prairie, **parkway corridors** joining some of the existing state parks, scenic river areas, **bog** and nature areas, **wildlife refuges** and boat **access** areas.

Park areas are being developed to offer a wide variety of outdoor recreation. Several thousand new campsites, equipped with modern facilities, are being built continuously. There have been efforts to expand park facilities to include education programs, recreation programs for campers, and environmental education programs that work with county school districts.

Illinoisans, like people in other states, have often ignored the effect of industry on the environment. In recent years the state has come to realize that once

In which season would these people probably go camping?

the environment is changed or damaged through **industrialization,** it is lost forever. The importance of the natural environment to the physical and mental health of the people has been emphasized all across the nation in recent years, and most states have passed environmental laws to preserve this valuable **heritage.**

In Illinois, the Environmental Protection Act, passed by the Legislature in 1970, created three new agencies: the Environmental Protection Agency, the Pollution Control Board, and the Institute for Environmental Quality. Penalties for pollution **vio-**

Which season do you think this represents?

lators have been increased. Research surveys have
been made to determine the effect of pollutants on
the **aquatic** environment. Other studies have been
made on various kinds of air and water pollution, and
remedial measures taken where necessary. The environmental programs are working in Illinois, and
the state now has probably the strongest antipollu-
tion laws in the nation. What this means to the citizens of the state, and perhaps even more important,
to future generations of Illinoisans, is that there will
always be opportunity to enjoy the natural environment and to participate in enjoyable and healthful
outdoor recreation.

What season is this? What kind of fish has this person caught?

Don't let it get away!

We might consider these many parks and recreation areas as being among our most valuable heritages, and pause to say thank you to those people in our state's history who had the foresight to see that wise land conservation practices were established.

Have you visited any state parks or camping areas? Do you like to fish, hike, or take part in any other outdoor activities? If you visit one of Illinois' parks or recreation areas, will you do your part in helping to keep it clean and attractive? Remember, no one enjoys an area in which others have left a lot of ugly **litter,** so be a good citizen and help keep our environment neat and clean. Future generations of Illinoisans will thank you for it.

Turn to the data section of the book and see what additional information you can find on recreation in Illinois.

Chapter VIII
Government

The Illinois State Capitol in Springfield. Started in 1868, completed in 1888.

Old State Capitol at Vandalia.

Early Government

Whenever human beings form a **society,** government is a natural and **indispensable** part of it. Can you imagine what life would be like if there were no **government?** At first a government is made up of unwritten laws (codes of behavior) and later most of these are written down.

A source of **power** or **authority** must be created to **enforce** these laws. Some societies have tried to do away with authority or avoid it, but they have not had any success.

The earliest historic forms of government in Illi-

First State Capitol at Springfield.

nois, that is those that we have written records of from the early explorers, were those of the Illini, the Potawatomi, Miami, Winnebago and Ottawa Indian tribes. The Sauk, Fox and Kickapoo Indians moved into Illinois early in the eighteenth century. There were prehistoric (before written records) societies in Illinois and they appear to have had governments similar to those of the historic Indians.

Our earliest written records of the Indian governments come from the French explorers and fur traders. The French got along well with the Indians and they sided with the French in the French and

A representative of the United States Government induces the Indians to sign away their land in exchange for more "fire water," (whiskey).

Indian war. This put the Indians on the losing side, and they were again on the losing side in the American Revolution.

In their contacts with the Indians, the white men always considered their own government, and, in fact, their whole society, to be **superior** to the Indian government and society. Once settlement began, the white government was stronger because of power or threat of power by its armies and weapons of war.

The whites and Indians had difficulty in understanding each other's governments. This meant that the whites often **forced** decisions on the Indians that were not popular with them. The Indians in turn were unable to seek **compromises** with the white men.

Often one tribal chief was **induced** to agree to something which affected other tribes that were allowed nothing to say about the matter. Ultimately the Indians gave up all their land in Illinois. Sometimes they were **tricked** out of their land. When they **resisted,** brief wars developed, with the Indians winding up the losers.

The following diagram and description will give you some idea of how the Illini government operated. This information is also true to some degree for other Indian governments. To get more information about these systems of tribal government, consult the resource and reference books or community resource people who are knowledgeable on the subject.

The outer circle suggests that everything within it is called a nation (six Illini tribes). Each of the six tribes had its own government, and all were united by a larger unit of government called a **tribal council.** This system resembled our own nation's organization of states into a federal government, except that the tribal council had much more control over the individual tribes. For this reason the organization of the Illini Nation is called a **confederation.**

A Tribal Government

The basic unit of each tribe's government was the **clan.** The tribes were divided into a number of groups based on family descent from father to son, like our own families. Also, like our families, the

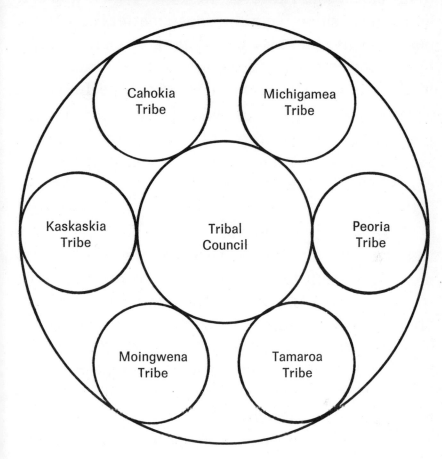

Indians did not marry within their own clan, but chose their brides or husbands from other clans.

Each clan took the name of a special animal or thing to which they felt related. This is called a **totem.** Thus there was a Thunder Clan, a Bald Eagle Clan, an Elk Clan, and so forth.

The head of each clan was an **hereditary** chief. That is, the title of chief was passed from the father

237

to his oldest son. However, the other men of the clan also had considerable influence in matters of war and peace, so the chief had to lead more by example than by the power of his office. Often this was more trouble than it was worth and the post was declined.

A **council** of the clan chiefs ruled each tribe. Its job was to decide matters of tribal **policy.** In order for the council to reach a decision, most of the clan chiefs would have to agree on the proper course of action.

Disputes among the various members of the tribe were handled informally. Thomas Forsyth, a government agent sent to arrange a peace conference with the Indians in 1812, reported that among the Indians "there is no such thing as a summary mode of **coercing** the payment of debts, all contracts are made on honor. For **redress** of civil injuries, an **appeal** is made to the old people of both parties and their determination is generally acceded to."

In case of a murder or attack by one member of the tribe on another, the guilty party was punished in a manner common to many **primitive** people. He was made to make payments or give presents to the relatives of his victim. Do you think such punishment would be effective today, at least for lesser crimes?

Even warmaking was handled informally by the tribe. A brave who could **persuade** others to follow him could become a **temporary** war chief.

The tribal council of each Indian nation met in

June of each year—oftener if necessary. For the Illini, the meeting was held at Kaskaskia, a village of almost 500 lodges. The tribal council was more like a **convention,** or a Scout jamboree, than a modern legislature's meeting. Sometimes as many as 8,000 Indians came to some of the larger meetings.

There was a large **ceremonial** lodge for the chiefs, **medicine men** and other leaders of the tribes, but, of course, there were no hotels. This meant that the visitors to the tribal council meeting had to camp out around the village.

Besides the members of the nation, these visitors sometimes included **delegates** from other nations or tribes who had come to deal with the tribal council. These delegates were sometimes from the white man's government as well as from Indian nations.

At the tribal council meeting, the chiefs and leaders of the tribes settled the problems confronting the Indian nation. They also met with the representatives of other nations, both Indian and white. The decisions of the tribal council were generally accepted as law.

State Government

Our Illinois state government is patterned after the Federal Government with three branches. These are the **Legislative, Executive,** and **Judicial.**

The LEGISLATIVE BRANCH is made up of two houses, the House of Representatives and the Senate. The members of these "houses" are called State Rep-

ILLINOIS STATE GOVERNMENT

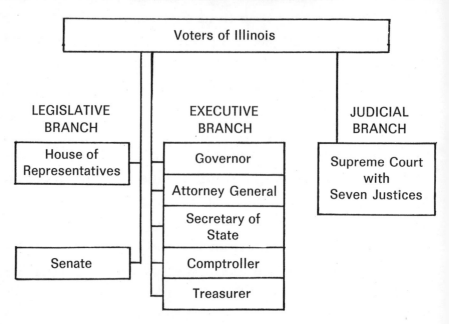

resentatives and State Senators. Both houses meeting together are called the **State Legislature** or the **General Assembly.**

Illinois is divided into fifty-nine legislative districts of as near equal population as possible. From each district one senator and three representatives are elected on even-numbered years. The representatives serve two-year terms and the senator serves two four-year terms and one two-year term.

The representatives are elected by a system called **cumulative voting,** which is **unique** to Illinois. Each voter has three votes for representative and may give all of them to one candidate, one and a half

240

votes each to two of the candidates, or one vote to three **candidates.** The three candidates who get the most votes are elected to two-year terms in the House of Representatives.

The General Assembly meetings start on the second Wednesday of each year and continue until the legislators have completed all the work before them. Most of this work is the making of laws for Illinois. However, the General Assembly may also submit **amendments** to the Illinois Constitution to the voters of the state, or may vote on an amendment to the United States Constitution submitted to the states by Congress. The Senate must **confirm** a governor's appointments of public officials. In rare cases the General Assembly may **impeach** (bring charges against) state officials.

Special sessions of the General Assembly may be called by either the Governor or the Senate President and Speaker of the House.

The EXECUTIVE BRANCH of Illinois is headed by the Governor. He is assisted by the Lieutenant Governor, the Attorney General, the Secretary of State, the Comptroller and the Treasurer. The Governor and the Lieutenant Governor run as a team as do the President and the Vice President of the United States. The other executive officers run separately.

The election of executive officers of Illinois is now in a period of gradual **transition** to the state's fourth constitution which went into effect on July

Course of a Bill

A bill may originate in either House or Senate, and the procedure is almost identical. If it originates in House:

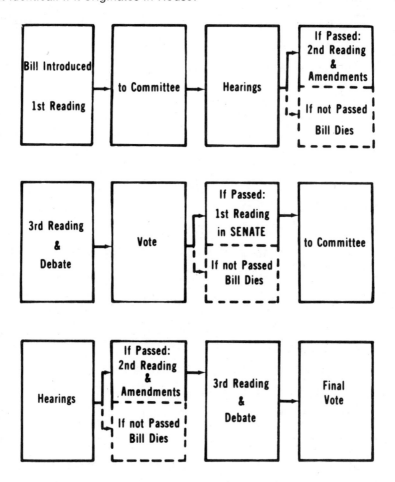

If Senate does not amend original House bill—the bill then goes to the Governor for his approval. Governor may sign bill, or allow bill to become law without his signature—or Governor may veto the bill.

If Senate amends bill, it goes back to House. If House concurs in Senate amendments, the bill goes to the Governor for his action.

If Senate amends bill, it goes back to House. House may refuse to accept amendments. If Senate withdraws amendments, bill goes to Governor for action. If Senate will not withdraw amendments, bill goes to Conference Committee where differences may be worked out. If agreement is reached by both Houses, bill then goes to Governor for action.

If after amended the bill is rejected by House, and either House or Senate fails to approve report of Conference Committee, bill may go to a second Conference Committee to work out difference. If either House or Senate does not approve the Conference Committee report, the bill is then dead.

HOW A STATE LAW MAY BE CHANGED

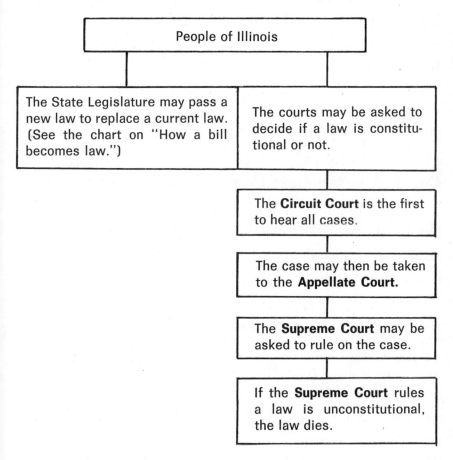

1, 1971. As this constitution explains: "The Governor, Lieutenant Governor, Attorney General, Secretary of State, and Comptroller elected in 1972 shall serve for four years and those elected in 1976 for two years. The Treasurer elected in 1974 shall serve for four years." After that, all of the state's elected executive officers will be elected every four years, starting in 1978.

243

The principal duty of the executive branch of Illinois' government is to carry out the laws passed by the legislature and to uphold the provisions of the state and national constitutions. The officers of this branch cannot make laws, but they can and do make **recommendations** to the state legislature.

The JUDICIAL BRANCH is the court system of Illinois. There are three levels of courts in the state. From the highest on down these are: the **Supreme Court,** the **Appellate Court,** and the **Circuit Courts.**

The chief function of these courts is to determine the guilt or innocence of those charged with breaking state laws. They also determine whether or not state laws **violate** the State or Federal Constitution.

The Illinois Supreme Court is made up of seven justices (judges) each elected for a term of ten years. Three of the justices are selected from Cook County and one each from the other four judicial districts of the state. The seven justices choose one of their number as Chief Justice. The Supreme Court hears cases which cannot be decided in the lower courts.

There are nine divisions of the Appellate Court in Illinois, each with three judges elected for a ten-year term. Cook County has five of the divisions, and the other four judicial districts of the state each have one division of the Appellate Court. The Appellate Court is called by that name because it hears cases appealed to it from the Circuit Courts.

The Circuit Courts are the only **trial** courts in

Illinois. The state has twenty-one judicial circuits, each with a number of Circuit Judges who are each elected for six years. These judges select one of their number Chief Judge. The Chief Judge then assigns cases to the other Circuit Judges and appoints Associate Judges to four-year **terms** to hear other cases.

Judges are elected to their first term in the same manner as other state officeholders. However, if a judge wishes to serve additional terms, his, or her, name is put on a separate ballot without an opposing candidate. The voters are then asked, "Shall So-and-so be retained as Judge of the Circuit Court? Vote yes or no."

County Government

There are 102 counties in Illinois, each with its own government charged with making and enforcing the laws of that county. This government operates from one of the important towns, or cities, of the county. Here you will find a courthouse or county building. Most of the offices of the county are housed in this structure.

Each county elects a Sheriff, a County Clerk, and a Treasurer. Other officials, such as the Coroner, the Recorder, the Assessor, and the Auditor, are either elected or appointed, depending upon the state law and the county ordinance (law). The governing body for a county is the Board of Commissioners.

Seventeen of Illinois' counties have three commissioners each. These are elected **at large** from the

COOK COUNTY GOVERNMENT

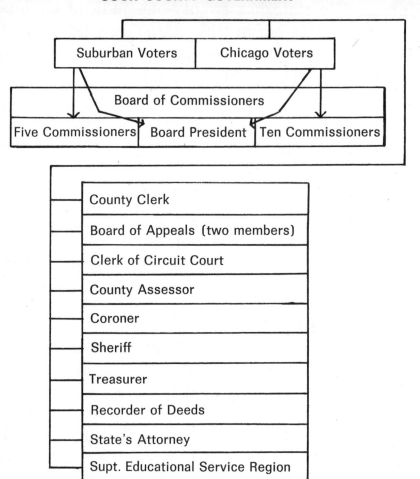

entire county, one being elected each year for a three-year term. Except for Cook County, which has a special form of government, the other counties are divided into townships. After each reapportionment election the supervisors draw lots and some serve four-year terms and others serve two-year terms. From then on half of the supervisors are elected to four-year terms on even-numbered years.

OTHER COUNTY GOVERNMENTS

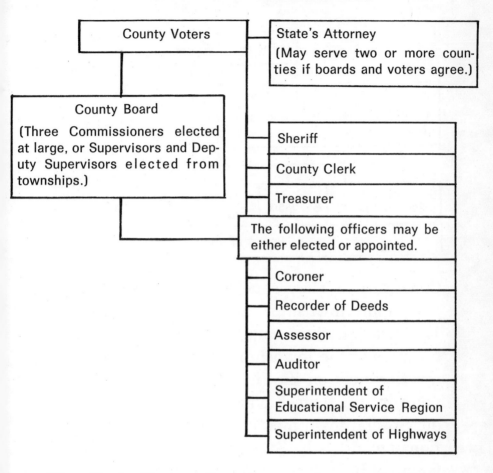

The Cook County Board is made up of fifteen members, ten elected from Chicago and five from the rest of the county. In addition, the President of the Cook County Board is elected at large from the county and is its chief executive officer. All sixteen are elected for four-year terms.

Townships

Townships were authorized by the 1848 Illinois

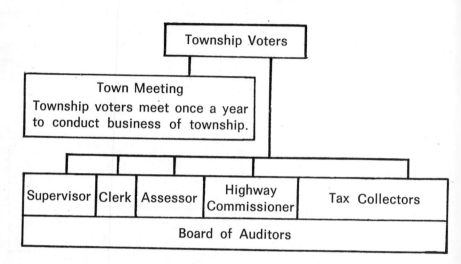

Constitution. They generally follow the line of the geographic townships laid out by the Ordinance of 1787, except where county boundaries interfere. The business of the township is carried out at an **annual meeting** held on the first Tuesday in April. All the voters of the township are eligible to attend, but few do. Special town meetings may be called by a **petition** signed by the Supervisor, the Clerk and fifteen voters of the township, for special cases.

The township officials are elected for four-year terms by the voters at an annual election which may be on the same day as the annual meeting, but not during it. Besides the Supervisor and the Clerk, the township officials include an Assessor, a Highway Commissioner and four members of the Board of Auditors. Tax collectors are elected in the townships of four counties.

TRUSTEE FORM

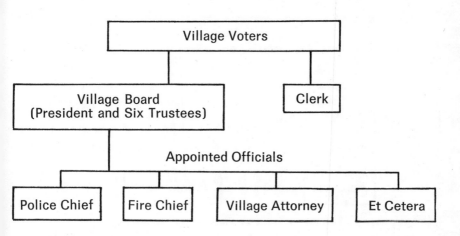

When a city or village's boundaries are the same as those of a township, the officers of the two may be combined. The Board of Auditors manages the township between town meetings. When there is no county health department, the township supervisor, the assessor and the clerk form a board of health. Other boards serve special purposes, such as libraries, parks, etc.

Municipal Government

"Municipalities," the Illinois Constitution says, "means cities, villages and incorporated towns." The voters of these municipalities can choose from among four forms of government:

The TRUSTEE FORM is used mostly by smaller towns and villages. In it a board of six trustees, a clerk and a president (who is often unofficially

249

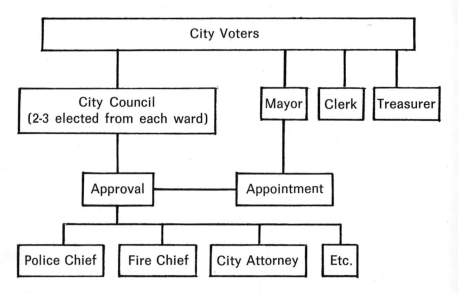

called a mayor) are elected every two or four years with half of the trustees being elected at a time.

The trustees are elected at large unless the town is over 25,000 population. The voters may then choose to elect the trustees from districts.

The President and trustees meet together as a board to make the laws for the town and to appoint other local officials. The village President votes only in case of a tie and may also **veto** the laws passed by the board. The veto may be **overridden** by a two-thirds vote of the trustees.

In the MAYOR-COUNCIL or ALDERMANIC FORM, a city is divided into wards. The number of wards depends on how many people there are in the city. Usually two aldermen are elected from each

250

COMMISSION FORM

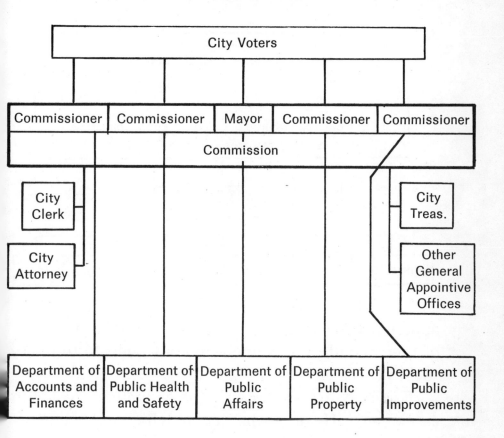

ward, or the council may also use the cumulative voting system of the General Assembly's House of Representatives, with three aldermen being elected from each ward. In either case, the aldermen are elected for four years, with their terms being staggered so that about half the council is elected every four years.

A Mayor, a Treasurer and a Clerk are elected from the city at large for four-year terms. The Mayor

251

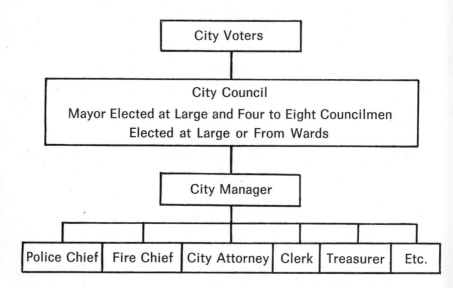

appoints the other city officials, with the approval of the council. The council may also decide to make these offices elective.

The Mayor **presides** over the council and votes in case of a tie. He or she has a veto which may be overridden by a two-thirds vote of the council.

In the COMMISSION FORM, a Mayor and four Commissioners are elected at large every four years. These five officials serve as both city council and heads of departments. Each Commissioner and the Mayor appoints the officers for his own department. All six meet regularly to pass the laws for the city.

The voters of the city may remove any Commissioner or the Mayor from office before his term is over. This is called **Recall.**

A petition signed by 10 percent of the voters may suggest a new law not passed by the council. This is called **Initiative.** If the council passes an unpopular law, it may be put to a vote of the people, called a **Referendum**, within thirty days, by a petition signed by 25 percent of the voters.

In the CITY MANAGER or MANAGERIAL FORM, the voters may choose between two different ways of electing their officials. They may elect the mayor and four to eight aldermen at large. Under this system the mayor may veto appropriations and veto in case of a tie or when a two-thirds or three-fifths vote is needed.

If the city is already divided into wards, the voters may choose to continue electing one or two aldermen from each ward and the mayor at large.

The council hires a professional city manager who appoints the department heads of the city and generally oversees the city government. He also reports to the city council and makes suggestions for programs to be carried out in the city.

The city council may fire the city manager and hire a new one any time they are dissatisfied with the work he is doing.

School Districts

Each of Illinois' school districts is **independent** of other local governments.

The governing unit of an elementary or unit school district of less than 1,000 people is a board of directors. Other school districts are governed by a board of education.

In either case, the organization is much like the city manager form. The members of the school district board are elected at large and hire a professional, the Superintendent of Schools. The Superintendent then operates the school system and reports back to the board.

Relationship Between State and Federal Governments

What powers does the Federal Government have and what powers do the state governments have? It does seem confusing, and it was confusing until our forefathers met in Philadelphia back in 1787.

They wrote a **document** that was to become perhaps the most famous the world has ever seen. This document is called the Constitution of the United States of America, and it defines clearly the function and power of the Federal Government and the function and power to be assumed by each state.

This document has enabled our nation to prosper and grow for over a hundred and eighty-eight years. Each of Illinois' four state constitutions has been patterned after the federal model, with changes to suit it to state government. However, the first three state constitutions lacked the federal model's ability to be changed to meet changing conditions. Hopefully Illinois' 1971 constitution will be more successful.

The following chart will show those powers given

■ Distribution of Constitutional Power

STATES MAY

Control elections, local governments, public health, safety and morals, within their boundaries (includes such things as marriage, divorce, education and general voting qualifications).

STATES MAY NOT

Interfere with functions of the federal government, such as making war, writing treaties with foreign countries, maintaining armies or navies, printing their own money.

FEDERAL GOVERMENT MAY

Regulate commerce over state lines and with foreign nations. Ratify treaties and carry on foreign relations. Maintain postal systems, grant copyrights, coin money, declare war, and raise, support and make rules for the regulation of an army and navy.

FEDERAL GOV'T MAY NOT

Favor one state at expense of another. Grant titles of nobility, or restrict an individual from knowing the statement of charges against him or prevent him from the right of a speedy trial, except in cases of rebellion or invasion.

BOTH MAY

Levy taxes.
Build roads.
Borrow money.
Spend money for the general welfare.

BOTH MAY NOT

Deprive persons of life or property without due process of law, or pass laws incriminating persons for acts that were not illegal when committed.

to the Federal Government and those reserved for the states. It will show what each government can and cannot do.

Citizens' Responsibilities to Their Government

No democratic form of government can survive unless its citizens carry out their responsibilities to it. Each person has been given a **role** to play in this process. If each citizen takes the role seriously, he will continue to enjoy the benefits of a government that is responsive to his own needs and wishes. The individual citizen has many **responsibilities** to his various governments, some of which are:

1. To obey the laws his government (local, state and national) has established.
2. To vote for officials who will speak for him and carry out his feelings in matters of legislation.
3. To keep informed of problems and issues of the day, on local, state and national levels, in order to vote intelligently.
4. To share in the cost of operating government by paying his fair share of taxes at all levels of government.

Can you think of other responsibilities that a citizen in our democratic society might have?

Many years ago, near the end of the Civil War in America, President Lincoln gave a speech near the Gettysburg, Pennsylvania, battlefield. In this speech he referred to our government as ". . . of the people,

The Citizen's Role In Government.

by the people and for the people . . ." What do you
think this quotation means?

The following diagram may help you understand
the several roles a citizen plays in the various types
of government under which he lives. Note that the

citizen is placed at the center of the diagram and that he is enclosed by circles representing the increasing size of the units of government to which he belongs.

Chapter IX

Who's Who in Illinois History

Civil War Generals from Illinois

Benjamin H. Grierson

John A. Logan

John A. McClernand

Ulysses S. Grant

Stephen A. Hurlbut

Richard J. Oglesby

John M. Palmer

What Makes a Person Famous?

Have you ever thought why we put the label **"famous"** on some people in our society? Is it because they managed to get their names in the news a lot? Is it because they are wealthy? Is it because they are great speakers or writers or leaders? Perhaps these are reasons in some cases, but there is a more important reason. Let's see if we can find out what it might be.

There are many **qualities** that tend to make a person famous in his society. Often a person is not recognized for his **achievements** in his own lifetime, but many years later these achievements take on added meaning. A new **generation,** looking back through the time of history, can judge the **contributions** of individuals or groups.

Famous is a word that must be measured in degrees. Some people are considered famous for one contribution or achievement, while others may be famous for many. Some people may be considered famous for a seemingly unimportant accomplishment and others for accomplishments of far greater importance. Perhaps the best **criteria** for judging a person's fame is to ask the question: "Did this person do anything in his lifetime that benefited the society to which he belonged?" (Did he help his fellow man?)

The social group or society that we are concerned with here is that composed of Illinois residents, past

261

and present. The list contains names of those who have contributed something to our state. There may be some people on the list who did more harm to society than good. You will have to judge that for yourself. Even though a person might do more to hurt a society than to help it, can he still be called famous? Perhaps you can find a word other than famous to describe this sort of person.

There are many, many more names that could be added to this list, but space will permit only a few. The people selected for this list come from all walks of life and represent contributions in many fields. They are a part of Illinois history, and it is hoped that you will try to learn about as many of them as possible.

The "One-a-Day" Research Plan

Try the "one-a-day" research plan for finding out about the people on the list. Make an effort to look up information on one of these people each day until you have gone completely through the list. Jot down a few brief notes that will tell you what each person is noted for.

Some Examples to Get You Started

Five people from the list are described in the following sketches. Read these short sketches and find out why these people were considered "famous" in our state's history.

Olof Krans

Olof Krans was a resident at the Swedish colony of Bishop Hill. From his arrival there in 1850, until 1896, he painted many local scenes that provided later generations of Illinoisans with a pictorial record of what life had been like in the **colony** of immigrants. In 1896, at the 50th aniversary of the colony, he presented the village with a collection of nearly one hundred paintings. His **primitive** style and clearness of detail mark his works as valuable historical documents and provide one of the most important records of pioneer life ever assembled in any part of the country.

Some historians feel that in the faces of the people appearing in his paintings he has portrayed the stern, hard life of the pioneer and the determination that enabled them to make their new life in America. The early residents of Bishop Hill have been gone for many years, but their contributions to a new state will continue to live through the efforts of this talented Swedish artist.

Many of his paintings can be seen today where they are housed in the Colony Church at Bishop Hill. The Swedish National Gallery restored some twenty of his paintings in 1969, and other of his works can be seen in the Kennedy Gallery of New York, and the Chicago Historical Society, as well as in many private collections across the country.

263

Jane Addams

Jane Addams was born and grew up in Cedarville, Illinois. Her father ran the mill there and had served in the state legislature with Lincoln.

Jane was called Jenny when she was little. She had typhoid fever and then tuberculosis of the spine and was left with a crooked back. She was pale and thin all of her childhood and held her head slightly to one side. She thought that she was very ugly. She became concerned with all ugly scenes.

When she went to town with her father, she worried about the ugly houses some of the children lived in. She was more concerned after she had graduated from Rockford Seminary and went to Europe. She saw terrible **slums** there, too, and ugly conditions in which the people had to live.

When she returned to America after two years in Europe, Jane and her friend Ellen Starr went to Chicago. The year was 1889, and the town was growing very fast. Most of the people had arrived from other lands. They could not speak English. They were living in crowded, dirty slums. Jane made up her mind what she wanted to do.

Jane bought the Hull mansion in the heart of the slums with money her father left her when he died. She fixed the house up. The children of the neighborhood watched the **renovation** and redecoration of the house. When the children were invited in to visit, they were surprised to find that Miss Addams could speak their languages.

Next, a day nursery was begun so that the mothers could leave their babies when they went to work. Classes were started in cooking and sewing. More were added in woodworking and art. Dances and concerts were held in the old mansion. Hull House was a very busy **community center.**

Miss Addams worked hard to get laws passed to improve housing and to provide clean drinking water. She worked to get parks and playgrounds and summer camps for the slum children.

In 1931, Jane Addams was honored by being the first woman to win the Nobel Peace Prize. When Jane died in 1935, Hull House had grown to many buildings, with many people helping their neighbors to become useful and productive citizens.

In 1963, when the Chicago Circle Campus was built, friends fought to keep Hull House from being torn down. It was saved and moved to the new university, and stands as a **monument** to the little girl from Cedarville who spent her life caring for the poor.

Marshall Field

Marshall Field is a very famous name in Illinois today. He was born in Conway, Massachusetts, on August 18, 1834. His family were farmers, and he knew very early in his life that he did not want to become a farmer like his father and grandfather had been. He wanted something more exciting. He got a job in a **dry goods** store. He continued to work in other stores as his family moved about.

When Field was 22, he went out West—to Chicago. Chicago was a frontier town with muddy streets and wooden sidewalks. He looked for a job, and found one with a dry goods firm called Cooley, Wadsworth and Company. The owners soon learned that Marshall Field was a good worker and the best salesman the store had. He was made a partner in the business.

Field then got the chance to go into partnership with Potter Palmer. This store was considered the best in the West.

When the Chicago fire started, Field moved a lot of his **merchandise** out of the area. He used wagons covered with wet blankets. He stored the things in a barn away from the fire. When the fire was over, everyone came to the barn to buy goods they needed to replace those lost in the fire.

Marshall Field then built his own store near the lake. He made a lot of money and shared it with the people in Chicago. He helped to build the University of Chicago. He also founded a museum of natural history. It is sometimes called the Field Museum.

Marshall Field and Company is still a successful store in Chicago and the suburbs today. You can buy all kinds of products and unusual things from many lands.

Carl Sandburg

Carl Sandburg was a poet, historian, novelist, journalist and **minstrel.** He was born in 1878 of Swedish immigrant parents. The second in a family of seven children, Carl helped **supplement** the family income by delivering newspapers and working as an office boy. When he finished the eighth grade in 1891, he worked as a milkman and as a porter in the Union Hotel barbershop.

When he turned nineteen, he spent several months riding trains across the country as a **hobo.** While doing this, he learned a great many folk songs, the beginning of his "American Songbag." He later served in the Spanish-American War, and later returned to Galesburg, where he worked his way through a period at Lombard College. His first book of verse, called "In Reckless Ecstasy," was published in 1904. He then turned to journalism and worked on several Chicago newspapers.

In 1914, his "Chicago" and other poems were published, and he won the Poetry Magazine's greatest poetry award. His next published works were also volumes of poetry, entitled "Chicago Poems" and "Cornhuskers." He also wrote about the 1919 race riots in Chicago and published a book of verse for children entitled "Rootabaga Stories." Later he wrote a two-volume work called "Abraham Lincoln: The Prairie Years."

He became so interested in the life of Abraham

Lincoln that he devoted the next few years to completing a four-volume work entitled "Abraham Lincoln: The War Years." This work won for him the world-famous Pulitzer Prize. Later works were called "Remembrance Rock," a novel, and a book called "Selected Poems."

In 1945, the Sandburgs moved to Flat Rock, North Carolina, and his next book, "Collected Poems," won a second Pulitzer Prize. Following his death in 1967, the beloved poet-historian's ashes were returned to his birthplace at Galesburg. The Carl Sandburg birthplace has been designated a state historic site, and each year many people from all across the country visit there and pay their respects to one of Illinois' most famous people. Many schools across the nation have been named in his honor. Is there a school in your town named for this famous person?

Peter Cartwright

The **circuit riders** were rugged men who smelled of wood smoke and saddle leather. Before the church was established in new regions, these men brought the word of God. They visited settlements in the furthermost regions, making the wilderness their **parish.** The most famous of these was Peter Cartwright.

Cartwright was a Methodist. He **converted** hundreds at the camp meetings. He was as well known for keeping order with his fists as for his **oratory,** according to folklore of that period.

Cartwright started a school at Pleasant Plains in 1830. In 1837, he helped Bishop McKendree found a **denominational** college at Lebanon, McKendree College.

Peter Cartwright was also a politician. He was elected twice to the Legislature and he ran for Congress one time. He lost that election. His winning opponent was Abraham Lincoln.

Famous People Associated With Illinois

Addams, Jane
Adler, Dankmar
Altgeld, John Peter
Anson, Adrian ("Cap")
Armour, Philip D.
Atkinson, Colonel Henry
Bacon, Samuel
Baldwin, Thomas Scott
Banks, Ernie
Benny, Jack
Birkbeck, Morris
Bickerdyke, "Mother"
Black Hawk
Bond, Shadrack
Borden, Gail
Boudreau, Lou
Breese, Sidney
Brooks, Gwendolyn
Brown, Mordecai
("Three Finger")
Bryan, William Jennings
Bryant, William Cullen
Burnham, Daniel
Cabrini, Frances Xavier
Camras, Marvin
Cannon, Joseph G.
Capone, Alphonse (Al)
Cartwright, Peter

Catherwood, Mary
Hartwell
Cermak, Anton J.
Chanute, Octave
Clark, George Rogers
Coles, Edward
Comiskey, Charles
Compton, Arthur H.
Cook, Daniel Pope
Crothers, Rachel
Cudahy, John
Daley, Richard J.
Darrow, Clarence
Davis, David
Davisson, Clinton Joseph
Dawes, Charles Gates
Deere, John
De Fleurville, William
De Forest, Lee
Decatur, Stephen
De Priest, Oscar
De Soto, Hernando
Dirksen, Everett M.
Dix, Dorothea
Dixon, John
Douglas, Paul H.
Douglas, Stephen A.
Duncan, Matthew

Duncan, Joseph
Duryea, Frank
Du Sable, Jean Baptiste
Earp, Wyatt
Edwards, Ninian
Eifert, Virginia
Faber, Urban C.
Fell, Jesse W.
Fermi, Enrico
Ferris, George W. G.
Field, Eugene
Field, Marshall
Flower, George
Flower, Lucy
Funk, Gene
Garland, Hamlin
Glidden, Joseph
Goldberg, Arthur J.
Goodman, Benny
Grange, Harold ("Red")
Grant, Ulysses S.
Gunn, C. L.
Halas, George
Hall, James
Harper, William Rainey
Harrison, William Henry
Hay, John
Hansberry, Lorraine
Hartnett, Charles
  ("Gabby")
Heacock, B. C.
Hearst, William Randolph
Hemingway, Ernest
Henry, Marguerite
Hickok, "Wild Bill"
Hillman, Sidney
Horner, Henry
Hornsby, Rogers
Hubbard, Elbert
Ickes, Harold L.
Ives, Burl

Janssen, Erik
Jenney, William La Baron
Joliet, Louis
Jones, Mary Harris
  ("Mother")
Judson, Clara Ingram
Kelley, Florence
Knox, Frank
Krans, Olof
Krupa, Gene
Lafayette, Marquis de
La Salle, Sieur de
Lathrop, Julia C.
Lawson, Victor F.
Lewis, John Llewellyn
Lincoln, Abraham
Lindbergh, Charles A.
Lindsay, Vachel
Logan, John A.
Lovejoy, Elijah
Lovejoy, Owen
Lowden, Frank O.
Luckman, Sid
Lundy, Benjamin
Lyons, Theodore A.
Marquis, Don
McCormick, Cyrus Hall
McCormick, Robert R.
McGee, Fibber and Mollie
McLean, John
McLeish, Archibald
Manny, J. H.
Marquette, Father Jacques
Masters, Edgar Lee
Mayer, Oscar
Medill, Joseph
Meigs, Merrill C.
Menard, Pierre
Michelson, Albert A.
Millikin, Robert A.
Monroe, Harriet

Moody, Dwight Lyman
Mueller, Hieronumous A.
Ogden, William B.
Oglesby, Richard
O'Hare, Lt. Edward H.
  ("Butch")
O'Leary, Mrs. Patrick
O'Neill, Mrs. Lottie Holman
Palmer, Potter
Palmer, John M.
Parsons, Louella
Peck, John Mason
Pfiester, Lester
Pinet, Father Pierre
Pontiac
Pope, Nathaniel
Powell, John Wesley
Prophet
Pullman, George M.
Rainey, Henry
Renault, Phillipe
Reynolds, John
Root, George F.
Rosenwald, Julius
Sandburg, Carl
Saperstein, Abe
Sayers, Gale
Seeley, John
Segar, Elza
Senachwine
Shabbona
Sheen, Fulton J.
Shelton Brothers

Shields, James
Sinclair, Upton
Smith, Joseph and Hyrum
Spaulding, Albert G.
Stevenson, Adlai E. I, II, III
Sullivan, Louis Henry
Sunday, William A.
Swift, Gustavus
Taft, Lorado
Thomas, J. W. E.
Thomas, Theodore
Thompson, William Hale
  ("Big Bill")
Todd, Mary
Tolton, Father Augustine
Tonti, Henri de
Tucker, Preston T.
Turner, Jonathan Baldwin
Urey, Harold C.
Van Doren, Carl
Van Doren, Mark
Van Dyke, Dick
Walker, Daniel
Ward, A. Montgomery
Willard, Francis E.
Willard, Frank
Williams, Dr. Daniel Hale
Wilson, Thomas
Wright, Frank Lloyd
Wright, John Stephen
Wrigley, Philip K.
Yerkes, Charles Tyson
Young, Brigham

Chapter X
Illinois' Problems Today

There have been problems all through Illinois' history. Problems of one period may be entirely different from those of another period. Transportation (or lack of it) was a problem in early-day Illinois. It is still a problem, but for different reasons. Can you think of possible explanations for this? No society can exist without facing up to its problems, and it is the successful society that solves its problems. Illinois today is faced with many problems, and we will look at some of them in an effort to see what can be done or is being done to solve them.

Housing is a problem in Illinois. How do we provide enough houses for our people, and at a price they can afford? Where should we build houses? Do we tear down older buildings or do we take up thousands of acres of productive farmland and build houses there? Do we build inside the large cities or do we go out to the **suburbs** to build? Should we build entirely new cities?

Should we build comfortable homes for those in our society who may be **unemployed** or **handicapped** in some way? Should we make it possible for all members of our society to become homeowners by passing **legislation** that will solve some of the problems involved? Should we permit individuals to build a home anywhere or should there be some **restrictions** set up by the society to regulate this building? Should we permit people of all races and

What is happening to our air?

Is there such a thing as "people pollution?"

ethnic groups to buy or rent homes wherever they choose?

Add some questions of your own to this list and attempt to answer them in terms of your own personal opinion and conviction.

Transportation is a problem in Illinois as mentioned earlier. Do we have enough good highways connecting all parts of the state? Can we afford to build new highways? Who pays for them? Are there too many cars on our highways today? Too many trucks? Do these vehicles contribute to **air pollution?** Is it safe to travel on our present highways? How could they be made safer? What are the major causes of death on our highways?

Is our present railroad system adequate in terms of passenger service both within the state and to other parts of the United States? In terms of freight service? Why has the railroad industry **declined** over the past ten to twenty years? Do airports contribute to air pollution? To **noise pollution?** What can be done to solve these problems?

Add questions of your own to this list for consideration.

Taxation is a problem in Illinois. Are Illinoisans paying too much in terms of the number of taxes they pay? Why are **taxes** necessary? Who pays taxes in Illinois? Should everyone pay an equal amount of tax? What does the state legislature do to raise money for the operation of the state government?

Where do our county governments get their money to operate? Where do cities and villages get money for their purposes? Where do schools get their money? What is a **"taxpayers' revolt"**? Should Illinoisans view taxpaying as a privilege or a painful duty? What are some possible new **sources** of obtaining tax money? Is the Illinois State Lottery a good way of raising money?

Add questions of your own to this list for consideration.

Education is a problem in Illinois. Can we afford to build new schools fast enough to meet the demands of fast-growing areas? Is it possible to build too many schools? Where should schools be built? Should schools be open the year round or merely for nine months of the year? Should schools do more than they are now doing to help students with special learning problems?

Should every school district have a **vocational-technical school**? Should all students be required to finish twelve years of education? Who provides most of the tax money for schools? What is **state aid** to schools and where does this money come from?

Add questions of your own to this list and attempt to find answers to as many as possible.

The environment, or rather the **preservation** of our environment, is affected by many problems today. What is to be done with solid waste and garbage in our cities? How is it disposed of now? How do

A dumping area in the sky.

Petroleum can be refined. How about air?

Sewage is still being dumped into our rivers. Why?

Is there a better way?

present **disposal** methods affect the environment? Some people engaged in environmental study say that our factories, power plants and automobiles are pouring **pollutants** into our atmosphere (and water) at such a rate that human life is in danger. What do you think will be done in the future to solve this problem? What is your community doing to protect the environment?

Insecticides and pesticides are being used in such quantity and in such powerful form that our wildlife and perhaps our own lives are in danger. Some agricultural experts tell us that in order to grow enough food to feed the world, we must continue to use these products to protect the crops. Some health authorities insist that life cannot exist after widespread use of these chemicals reaches a **saturation point.** This is truly a **dilemma.** What should be done to resolve the problem? What has your own community done in regard to the problem of **insecticides** and **pesticides?**

Illinois' rivers and lakes (true in other states as well) are being used as dumping areas for factory and **municipal** disposal systems. The once pure, clean water the early explorers and voyageurs took from these water sources to drink is no longer fit. In some cases, fish, birds and plant life have died as a result of the "poisoned" water. What will be done in the future about this serious situation? What is the state government doing at the present to help solve the problem? What is your own community doing?

What do you think happened to this water area? Who would benefit if it were to be cleaned up?

What happened to this lakeshore?

Where does your community get its supply of drinking water?

Much of the wetlands or swampy areas of the state have been drained to provide more land for farming. This has taken away bird and animal "**habitat**" and caused our wildlife supply to shrink in number. What is being done by the state government to cope with this problem? Does your community have such a problem? Will this continue to be a problem in future years?

Drug abuse is a major problem in Illinois, just as in other states. Often the thrill of trying something **daring** or **forbidden** causes young people to **experiment** with drugs. This experimentation often leads to ill health, mental disorders and sometimes death. The person who becomes **addicted** to any drug may soon find himself at the mercy of a "**pusher**," who wants cash for his illegal product. This need for money often prompts an **addict** to turn to crime in order to pay for his expensive **habit**. Once-happy families often break up because of problems and pressures brought on by drug use and abuse. Is it worth the price?

How many drugs can you think of that are a problem or danger in your own community? Where do they come from? Is there a drug education program in your school? In your community? What more could be done to make people aware of the dangers? Is **marijuana** a drug? What is the penalty for having

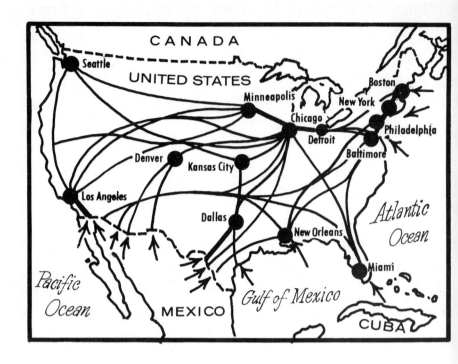

Drug traffic routes in the United States.

this substance in one's possession? Has there always been a drug problem in Illinois?

Population decline is another problem for Illinoisans to consider. Each year we find that more and more people leave the farms of the state and move to the cities. This loss of **rural** population leaves fewer family owned farms and often leaves many vacant farm buildings that rapidly become **dilapidated** monuments to the past. Why do people leave the farms? Where do they go and what do they do to earn a living? What can be done to encourage these people to stay on their farms? Should they be en-

Did they have to die?

How do you catch a "Litter Bug?"

couraged to stay on the farm? Is anything being done about this problem, to your knowledge?

Many small towns in Illinois lose population each year. There has been a **population shift** from smaller towns to larger towns and cities. What problems does this cause for both the town losing the population and the city or suburb gaining the population? What are suburbs? Why are they growing? Should people be encouraged to remain in small towns? What would encourage them to stay?

Other Problems

We have posed questions concerning a few of the problems facing our state today. There are many more that could be discussed if space permitted. Perhaps you can add some more to the list and think of reasons why they should be called problems.

You might also think through several possible solutions to these problems and try to find out what, if anything, is being done in your community to solve them. Try to classify your list of problems under the headings of **environmental problems** or **social problems.** Is it possible for a problem to be listed under both headings?

Turn to the data section of the book (miscellaneous section) and see if you can find some things that could be called problems in Illinois.

Chapter XI

Looking Back:
How Social Scientists Would
Look at Illinois

Cardinal by Richard Sloan
Courtesy of Griggsville Wild Bird Society

Meadowlark by Richard Sloan
Courtesy of Griggsville Wild Bird Society

Red-Tailed Hawk by Richard Sloan
Courtesy of Griggsville Wild Bird Society

Prairie Chicken by Richard Sloan
Courtesy of Griggsville Wild Bird Society

Brown Thrasher by Richard Sloan
Courtesy of Griggsville Wild Bird Society

Robin by Richard Sloan
Courtesy of Griggsville Wild Bird Society

Yellow Shafted Flicker by Richard Sloan
Courtesy of Griggsville Wild Bird Society

Black Capped Chickadee by Richard Sloan
Courtesy of Griggsville Wild Bird Society

Mallards by Richard Sloan
Courtesy of Griggsville Wild Bird Society

Great Horned Owl by Richard Sloan
Courtesy of Griggsville Wild Bird Society

Bob White by Richard Sloan
Courtesy of Griggsville Wild Bird Society

Ring-Necked Pheasant by Richard Sloan
Courtesy of Griggsville Wild Bird Society

American Goldfinch by Richard Sloan
Courtesy of Griggsville Wild Bird Society

River Otter by Richard Timm
Courtesy of Griggsville Wild Bird Society

Badger by Richard Timm
Courtesy of Griggsville Wild Bird Society

Bob Cat by Richard Timm
Courtesy of Griggsville Wild Bird Society

Eastern Cottontail by Richard Timm
Courtesy of Griggsville Wild Bird Society

Skunk by Richard Timm Courtesy of Griggsville Wild Bird Society

Black Eyed Susan
by Maryrose Wampler
Courtesy of Griggsville Wild Bird Society

Iris and Old Roses by Maryrose Wampler
Courtesy of Griggsville Wild Bird Society

Virginia deer in museum exhibit of an eastern Illinois hardwood forest, with spring flowers and bird migrants of early May.

Courtesy of Illinois State Museum

The unglaciated northwestern corner of Illinois before 1800. Museum exhibit showing elk, red squirrel, and ruffed grouse, all of which have disappeared from Illinois; and the birch and aspen trees and rock ferns still surviving among the jagged limestone rock terrain.

Museum exhibit showing old beaches of Lake Michigan which formed sand ridges inhabited by special plants and animals. Man has completely eliminated this habitat in Illinois except for a small section, "Illinois Beach Nature Preserve," near Zion, Illinois. The bear disappeared from Illinois in about 1850.

Museum exhibit showing the Grand Prairie of Illinois before 1800, with typical plants and animals, many of which were forced to give way to modern agriculture.

Museum exhibit showing grey or timber wolves on a sandstone ledge in the Shawnee Hills of southern Illinois pricr to 1890.

Museum exhibit showing the Canada Geese which gather by the thousands each fall in the Cypress and Tupelo Lakes of southern Illinois near Cairo. This is Horseshoe Lake.

History is sometimes called the memory of man's experiences. If it is forgotten or goes unnoticed, society may decline or fail. Without history and tradition, a society has no knowledge of what it is or how it came to be. The events of history have caused all the emotions, values, ideals and goals that make life have meaning. These things give people something to live for, struggle for and sometimes die for. Events of history have created countries, governments, religions and social classes that all work together to influence present-day society. Illinoisans today should view their state's past in order to understand and appreciate the heritage that has been passed from earlier generations.

To fully understand a group of people (a society), it is important that they be studied through the various branches or disciplines of social science. The areas we will deal with in the following pages are: **history, sociology, cultural anthropology, political science, economics,** and **geography.** Each of these areas of social science calls for special study and attention.

The Historian is mainly concerned with recording what happened, when it happened, where it happened, and what the results were. He is concerned with the following key words: **time, period, happening, cause, result, chronology,** and **change.**

The historian asks these questions:
1. What caused this particular event to take place?

2. Were there people involved who could have changed the final result?
3. Were there new ideas or inventions that caused the change?
4. How did the people feel about the issue or event?
5. Was the physical environment a factor in the issue or event?

The Cultural Anthropologist is concerned with studying a group of people (a society) to discover ways in which people are alike and ways in which they are different. He is interested in the ways the group meets its needs, and this he calls their "culture."

He is concerned with the following key words: **mankind, culture, values, beliefs,** and **acculturation** (spread or exchange of culture).

He asks the following questions:
1. What is man?
2. How does man differ from other creatures?
3. What are the major needs of this group?
4. What seems to be their way of life with regard to their values and beliefs?
5. What effect does physical environment have on their developed culture?
6. How does this culture meet the requirements for surviving?

The Political Scientist is interested mainly in political leadership. This involves the people or groups who make and enforce the laws or rules under which the political system operates. He is concerned with these key words: **authority, power, influence, government, decision-making,** and **leadership.**

He asks the following questions:

1. How many are involved in the process of choosing political leaders?
2. What does the society look for in people who are selected to fill leadership roles?
3. Who takes part in making political decisions?
4. How does the society determine how much authority to give to its leaders?

The Economist studies how the people in a society make choices and how they distribute resources to obtain needed products and services. He is concerned with these key words: **wants, needs, scarcity, exchange, production, distribution,** and **consumption.**

He asks the following questions:

1. What goods and services are produced?
2. How are goods and services produced?
3. For whom are these goods and services produced?
4. How much or in what quantity are they produced?
5. How fast has the economy grown?
6. What regulations have been developed to control this growth?
7. How does scarcity influence the occupational and technological status of this society?

The Geographer is mainly concerned with the plants, animals and minerals that make up the area to be studied. He wants to find out what happens when certain plants, animals, climate conditions, and people with a particular culture are found in an area. He wants to study the effect of environment on the people and to what extent the people have changed or adapted the environment to meet their goals.

He is concerned with the following key words: **place, location, area, environment, areal association.**

He asks the following questions:

1. How is this place different from other places?
2. How is it similar to other places?
3. Why are conditions the way they are in this place?
4. Did the people make any difference in these conditions?
5. Were natural resources important to this place?
6. How wisely were these resources used?
7. Do the people export raw materials or finished products?
8. What kinds of things do they receive from other places?
9. What kinds of activities do people take part in? Has it always been this way? Why?
10. To what extent has the terrain contributed to the overall progress of this place (or kept it from progressing)?

The Sociologist is concerned with how the people behave or act as they live in social groups. He wants to study cooperation and conflict among groups and what role the family, the school, the church, and the government have had in the growth of the society. He is concerned with social change, its cause, and its effect on the society. He also wants to study such things as crime, transportation, communication, and population distribution, as they have developed within the society. He wants to learn how this social group promotes loyalty to its beliefs, and how it has organized to protect itself from outside forces. He is concerned with the following key words: **group, social system, custom, conflict, interaction, role, norm, and sanction.**

He asks the following questions:

1. Why is this society organized as it is?
2. What systems have been created by this society?
3. What were the purposes and effects of these systems?
4. How do members of subgroups in this society feel toward each other?
5. Why do they feel this way?
6. What has happened to this society as it has been involved with population increase or decrease, automation and warfare?
7. Have the subgroups of this society all changed at the same rate?
8. How does this society regard its aged population?

9. In what ways does this society show an appreciation of culture and its inheritance?

Your Community

You have read about the various branches of social science and how each might be used in the study of a society. Using the same key words and questions that each social scientist would use, make a study of your own community and attempt to find out more about it by answering as many of the questions as possible. When you follow this plan of studying a community, a state, a nation, or any society, you are learning to look through the eyes of all the social scientists. To study only the historian's point of view, for example, would prevent you from gaining an appreciation of the society as viewed from the total social science perspective. Put on the glasses of the social scientist and see things as a total picture. Your understanding of and appreciation for a social group will be much more meaningful to you as a result.

A SUGGESTED MODEL FOR GATHERING AND ANALYZING DATA

The People

1. Where did they come from?
2. Why did they come?
3. What culture did they bring with them?
   a. Observances (religious, etc.)
   b. Food
   c. Clothing

    d. Political
    e. Economic
    f. Education

The Environment
4. What adaptations to the new environment had to be made in regard to:
    a. Food?
    b. Clothing?
    c. Shelter?
    d. Political?
    e. Economic processes (supply, demand, trade, scarcity, distribution, manufacture)?
    f. Education?

The Institutions
5. What patterns of change are evident in:
    a. Family?
    b. Government?
    c. Education?
    d. Religion?

Analysis and Generalization
6. In analyzing the data found for questions 1-5, what are some generalizations you might draw with regard to:
    a. Family?
    b. Government?
    c. Education?
    d. Religion?
    e. Shelter?
    f. Economic development?

Chapter XII

Touring Illinois:
Current Attractions and
Historic Sites

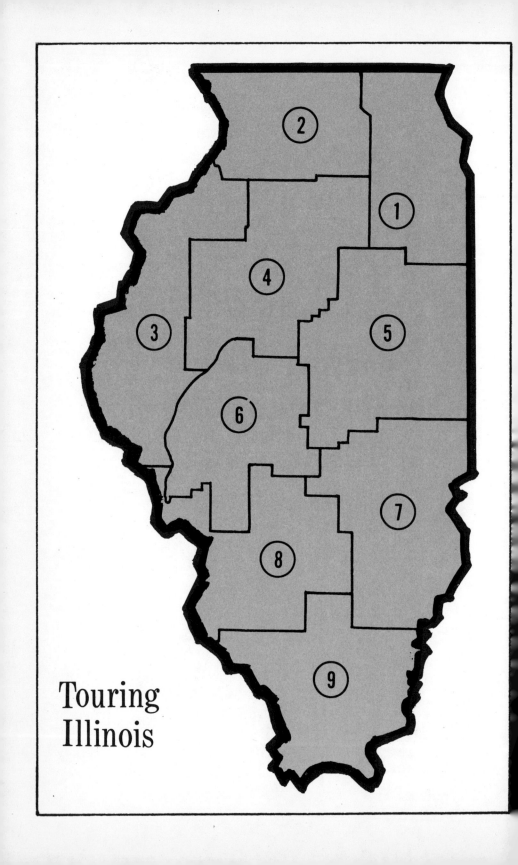

Touring
Illinois

ILLINOIS TOURISM AREAS
(Grouped by Counties)

Area One
Cook
Du Page
Grundy
Kane
Kankakee
Kendall
Lake
McHenry
Will

Area Two
Boone
Carroll
De Kalb
Jo Daviess
Lee
Ogle
Stephenson
Whiteside
Winnebago

Area Three
Adams
Brown
Hancock
Henderson
Henry
McDonough
Mercer
Pike
Rock Island

Schuyler
Warren

Area Four
Bureau
Fulton
Knox
La Salle
Marshall
Peoria
Putnam
Stark
Tazewell
Woodford

Area Five
Champaign
De Witt
Ford
Iroquois
Livingston
Macon
McLean
Piatt
Vermillion

Area Six
Cass
Christian
Greene
Logan
Macoupin
Mason
Menard

Morgan
Sangamon
Scott

Area Seven
Clark
Clay
Coles
Crawford
Cumberland
Douglas
Edgar
Edwards
Effingham
Jasper
Lawrence
Moultrie
Richland
Shelby
Wabash
Wayne

Area Eight
Bond
Calhoun
Clinton
Fayette

Jersey
Madison
Marion
Monroe
Montgomery
St. Clair
Washington

Area Nine
Alexander
Franklin
Gallatin
Hamilton
Hardin
Jackson
Jefferson
Johnson
Massac
Perry
Pope
Pulaski
Randolph
Saline
White
Williamson
Union

HISTORIC SITES

A Trip Around the State

Now that you have learned something about Illinois history, how would you like to take a make-believe trip around our state? Perhaps you have seen some of the interesting things in Illinois already.

Maybe your class could take a **field trip** to see some of the things in your area.

Area One

We will start our trip in Chicago, which is the transportation center of the nation. O'Hare Field is the busiest airport in the world. The Port of Chicago is busy, too. We will pretend though that we arrived by one of the many **expressways.** You can see all of the roads leading into Chicago as you look at a road map.

Chicago is nicknamed the Windy City. If you have ever been to Chicago, perhaps you will agree. The business area of Chicago is called "the Loop" because the **elevated trains** encircle the business area, making a loop. A five-story-tall **sculpture** by Pablo Picasso sits on the Civic Center **Plaza.** It is made of a special kind of steel so that it developed a protective rust covering. No one knows for sure what it represents. Some think it looks like a bird or perhaps a face. What do you think it is?

Chicago has many of the world's finest **museums,** zoos, art galleries and parks: the Museum of Science and Industry, the Field Museum of Natural History, the Chicago Historical Society, Adler **Planetarium**, Shedd **Aquarium**, Brookfield Zoo and Lincoln Park Zoo. A day could be spent at each one of these without seeing everything.

Chicago has many sporting events, too. Perhaps you know the name of the baseball, football, hockey, tennis and basketball teams there. Do you know some of the players on the teams?

Hull House is open and looks like it did when Jane Addams moved into it in 1889. There is a state **memorial** to Stephen Douglas, where he is buried, located near the site of the Douglas Home and the Civil War Camp Douglas.

North of Chicago is Evanston, with the homes of two famous Illinoisans. One is Charles Dawes, who was Vice President of the United States from 1925-1929, and the other is Frances Willard, a founder of the WCTU. Farther north of Chicago is Illinois Beach State Park where you can see Lake County and all the lakes created by long-ago glaciers.

Illinois has more than 80 state parks that are mainly recreation areas. Some are to preserve history of interesting people. A new park in this area is called Goose Lake Prairie. It preserves some of the last virgin prairie in the state. You can walk on a mile-long path through the park and see what Illinois looked like when the first settlers arrived. Also in this area in Grundy County is one of the largest trees in Illinois. It is an eastern cottonwood and has a **circumference** of 27 feet 4 inches, is 120 feet high and has a **crown** spread of 100 feet. Chief Shabbona, a Potawatomi who was a friend of the early settlers and refused to join Black Hawk, is buried here in Grundy County.

West of Chicago, in Du Page County, is the Morton **Arboretum,** which is an outdoor museum with 4,800 trees. Nearby, in Wheaton, is the Cantigny War Memorial, which has displays about World Wars I and II. Old Graue Mill in Hinsdale is an 1852 waterwheel gristmill which works, allowing you to see wheat changed to flour.

Waubonsee Creek in Kendall County has two **unique** features. It has the only known outcropping of Silurian Dolomite and Ordovician Maquokepa shale. **Fossilized** remains of prehistoric life called Oswegonenis Tentaculites are only found here and so were named for Oswego. Perhaps some of you "rock hounds" would be interested in seeing or finding these.

The last stop in Area I will be in Will County at the Illinois and Michigan Canal Museum. The canal was built in 1845 and connected the Illinois River with Lake Michigan. You can see two of the locks, the tollkeepers' house and the surgeon's office.

There are many more museums and interesting places to see in this area, but these will get you started.

Area Two

Area II, in the northwest corner of the state, has the highest point in Illinois, Charles Mound. It is 1,241 feet above sea level, and you can see three states from the top. What would they be? Look at a map to see.

General Ulysses S. Grant retired from the Army

in 1860 and took his wife and four children to Galena. Then came the Civil War, so Grant reentered the Army. He drilled the troops in Galena and took them to Springfield. He became the commander of all the Northern Army, and after the war, became President of the United States. To show their appreciation, the people of Galena gave him a home. The house has furniture, silver and china used in the White House. Also in Galena you can see the oldest remaining market house in the Midwest. Vinegar Hill lead mine is open to the public. In the 1820s, many miners came to Galena to try to make their fortunes. In the next **decades,** Galena was the lead mining capital of the world, and by the 1850s was producing 55 million pounds of lead ore.

There are two good statues of Lincoln in this area. The one in Dixon is called "Lincoln, a Young Volunteer." It shows Lincoln as he looked when he passed through Dixon in the Black Hawk War. One of the battles of the Black Hawk War was fought at Kent and is commemorated by a monument.

The other statue is in Freeport and is called "Lincoln, the Debater." Freeport was also the site of the second Lincoln-Douglas **debate** in 1858. North of Freeport is the **homestead** and tomb of Jane Addams.

Rockford is the second largest city in the state. (What is the largest?) There is a lot of manufacturing done in Rockford. The Erlander Museum is operated by the Swedish Historical Society and tells the story of the Swedish heritage in Rockford. There is also a rare Indian **effigy** mound along the Rock River. It is in the shape of a snake or serpent.

Farther south along the river at Oregon you can see a 40-foot-tall statue by Lorado Taft that idealizes the American Indian. It is made of reinforced concrete and was completed in 1911.

At Grand Detour, a village has been **reconstructed** around the blacksmith shop of John Deere. Remember, he made the first successful plow that speeded the opening of the prairie for farming.

Area Two is one of the most scenic in the state. Before Black Hawk gave up this land, which he lost at the Battle of Kellogg's Grove in the Black Hawk War, to the white people, he said, "It is a beautiful country. I loved my towns, my cornfields, and the home of my people. I fought for it. It is now yours. Keep it as we did."

Area Three

The counties along the Mississippi River in the western part of the state make up Area Three. Many of the towns are built on old Indian village sites. The area has a large Indian **heritage.** Blackhawk Park has an Indian **powwow** every Labor Day weekend. Also in Rock Island, but on Arsenal Island, is Fort Armstrong blockhouse **replica.** It is the site of the first permanent white settlement in the area in 1816. The Arsenal, which makes guns and ammunition, has been a busy place since Civil War times and is one of the largest **arsenals** in the world. There are two military cemeteries here, one of which is Confederate, since prisoners from the South were kept here during the Civil War. You can also visit the farm implement firms in the area.

Quincy was the site of the sixth Lincoln-Douglas debate. Its historical museum is housed in the home of a former Illinois governor, John Wood.

Pike County's first state representative, Nicholas Hansen, cast the deciding vote which kept Illinois from becoming a slave state. He was burned in effigy in Vandalia and the courageous vote cost him his political life.

There have been two interesting towns founded by early settlers in this area. One is Nauvoo and the other is Bishop Hill.

Joseph Smith had founded the Church of Jesus Christ of the Latter Day Saints and had brought his followers to Illinois in 1839. He founded a town called Nauvoo, which means Beautiful Place. The church, commonly called the Mormon church, sent out missionaries all over the world. The town grew very fast. By 1845, Nauvoo was the largest city in Illinois. Joseph Smith became interested in politics. He planned to run for president of the United States. Some of the people wondered how Smith had so much power. One newspaper wrote stories about his politics and ideas that made Smith angry. He and his brother Hyrum broke the printing press. They were put in jail in Carthage. Governor Thomas Ford had to call out the **militia** as the people were all upset. That didn't stop the **mob.** The mob broke into the jail and killed Joseph and Hyrum Smith. The new leader, Brigham Young, knew that he had to get the rest of the Mormons away. He led them to Salt Lake City, Utah. Their descendants live there today.

One can visit the jail at Carthage and Joseph Smith's home. There are other homes open, too, and the whole town is being restored. The temple built on the highest hill in Nauvoo has been destroyed.

After the Mormons left Nauvoo, the Icarians settled there. They were a French **communistic** religious community. They made wine and cheese. The Wedding of the Wine and Cheese festival is still held in Nauvoo every Labor Day weekend.

The settlers at Bishop Hill were Swedish. In 1846, when the settlers first arrived, they lived in hand-dug caves in the ground. The next spring they began construction of many three-story brick buildings. Brick houses were unusual, as other settlers were living in log cabins. The Steeple Building is interesting. It was first used as a school or hotel and has a one-handed clock on the steeple. The story goes that the minute hand fell off and the people were too busy to worry about minutes, and ever after the clock only had the hour hand.

Their church, where their leader, Erik Janssen,

gave many sermons, is open for visitors. The ground level of the church is a museum. It also has many paintings done by Olof Krans. He painted pictures of all the settlers and of the work that they did in the community, over a hundred altogether.

Monmouth was the birthplace of Wyatt Earp in 1848. Have you ever heard of him?

Area Four

The next area, number four, contains the sites of two Lincoln-Douglas debates. One was in Galesburg and the other at Ottawa.

Two famous poets were born or lived in this area: Carl Sandburg and Edgar Lee Masters. There were also two forts built by La Salle at Starved Rock and Fort Creve Coeur that are in this area. You will remember that Fort Creve Coeur, near Peoria, was built in 1680. The one called Fort St. Louis, at Starved Rock, was established in 1682. Remember, too, that Marquette and Joliet visited the Indians on the site of Starved Rock in 1673. Both places are now state parks.

Also near Peoria is the site of Jubilee College. The college was **chartered** in 1847, making it one of the first colleges founded in Illinois. It is also a state park now. Caterpillar Tractor Company, one of the largest employers in Illinois, is also in Peoria. Other industries there use the Midwest's grain to make breakfast cereal, livestock feed, and whiskey. On the courthouse square Lincoln **denounced** slavery for the first time publicly on October 16, 1854. Lincoln visited Metamora Courthouse for ten years when he was riding the circuit and serving as a lawyer.

North of Peoria is Princeton, which has one of the nine remaining covered bridges in Illinois. This one is painted red and you can drive through it in your car.

Also in Princeton is the home of Owen Lovejoy, where slaves were hidden on their way to safety in Canada. Owen was a brother of Elijah Lovejoy, who was killed by the angry mob in Alton.

Also in the area is the settlement of Norway, named by the pioneers for their homeland. Wild Bill Hickok, U. S. marshal, army officer and scout, was born in Troy Grove on May 27, 1837.

The birthplace of Carl Sandburg, biographer of Lincoln, is open in Galesburg. Here is part of one of his poems, called "Chicago."

Hog Butcher for the World,
Tool Maker, Stacker of Wheat,
Player with Railroads and the Nation's
    Freight Handler;
Stormy, husky, brawling,
City of the Big Shoulders.

Would you like to read the rest of his poem?

Nearby is Dickson Mounds Museum. Here you will see the skeletons of Indians who lived and died A.D. 900-1300. (How many years ago was that?) Some are buried with pottery and beads and other possessions. Sometimes a whole family was buried together. It is interesting because the skeletons are displayed just as they were found. Over a thousand skeletons have been found, and you can see 237 of them. There are many more burial mounds in the area that scientists are still working on. The museum also has exhibits telling the story of the Indians' life in Illinois at that time.

Area Five

Area Five is mainly agricultural and educational. Each year more than 60,000 students attend colleges and universities here. Perhaps you will go to college in this area. The University of Illinois has the most students in Champaign-Urbana. (The first state institution of higher learning is located at Normal and was founded in 1857.)

Bloomington is the county seat of McLean County. Do you remember who John McLean was? He was our first Representative in Congress. McLean is also the biggest county in the state. The first Pullman sleeping car was built in Bloomington, and the first commercially marketed hybrid seed corn was sold by Funk Brothers in 1916. The David Davis home is open in Bloomington, too. He was a friend of Abraham Lincoln's and was appointed by him to serve on the United States Supreme Court. Adlai Stevenson II, former governor, two-time candidate for President, and Ambassador to the United Nations, is buried in Bloomington.

There is much Lincoln lore in this area. The Lincolns lived ten miles west of Decatur when they first arrived in Illinois. Lincoln gave his first political speech in 1831 in Decatur, too. He practiced law in the courthouse there and was **endorsed** by Illinois Republicans as their candidate for President. At nearby Bement, in the Bryant Cottage, Lincoln and Douglas agreed to their series of debates.

Decatur is also the home of Richard Oglesby, the only three-time governor of the state.

Allerton Park at Monticello is noted for its famous **statuary** in an outdoor park setting. Also at Monticello is Voorhies Castle. The builder closed the house on the day his wife died, and nothing was disturbed. (Can you imagine going through your house fifty years from now? Do you think that they would think we had old-fashioned things?) The barn near the Voorhies Castle is also interesting because it has a big clock on it.

Area Six

The most important affairs of our state occur in Area Six. Our capital city is in this area, and the last two capitol buildings are here. Both buildings would be interesting for you to see.

The first that visitors to Springfield see of these buildings is the capitol dome rising 360 feet in the air. The building was finished in 1887, and cost $4,000,000. It is in the form of a Latin cross and is made of limestone, coming from several parts of the state. Inside is a statue called "Illinois Welcoming the World," and was brought to the capitol from the Illinois building at the World's Columbian Exposition. Nearby are the state museums, historical society, and other state buildings.

The Old State Capitol was recently reconstructed to look as it did when Lincoln served in the legislature in the building. Remember how he and the "Long Nine" worked to get the capital moved from Vandalia to Springfield? Lincoln gave one of his most famous speeches in the Old State Capitol. He said, "A house divided against itself cannot **endure,** permanently half slave and half free. I do not expect the Union to be **dissolved**—I do not expect the house to fall—but I do expect it will cease to be divided." Was he right?

Also in Springfield, at the corner of 8th and Jackson, is the only house Lincoln ever owned. He bought the house in 1844 for $1,500 with a $900 mortgage. Some of the furnishings in the house are original. The piano in the house was played at Lincoln's wedding.

Lincoln's Tomb is also in Springfield. In 1876, some thieves, led by Ben Boyd, a **counterfeiter,** tried to steal Lincoln's body. They had the casket out of the covering when they were captured. They had planned to sell the body to raise money.

New Salem, the town where Lincoln lived for six years, is nearby. The town was only inhabited for about ten years, and there were never more than a hundred people in New Salem. It became a **ghost town** when the captains of the steamboats found that the Sangamon River was too shallow for them to **navigate,** and the railroad bypassed the town by two and a half miles. The restored town has twelve cabins, ten shops, the Rutledge Tavern and a school. A post office is operated in the Lincoln-Berry store building, where Lincoln once served as postmaster. Sometimes you can ride around the park in a covered wagon pulled by oxen. There is a museum to visit and a steamboat to ride, and there is a country music show nearby.

Lincoln, Illinois, is the only town named for the President when he was alive. He supplied a wagon-load of watermelons to celebrate the naming of the town and **christened** the town with watermelon juice.

Two other Lincoln circuit-day courthouses, Mount Pulaski and Postville, are in this area. Lincoln was nicknamed "Honest Abe" at the one at Postville when he was riding the circuit.

The Clayville Stagecoach Inn has been restored, too. It was built in 1824, and housed many weary travelers riding the **stages.**

Edgar Lee Masters lived in Lewistown as a boy and is buried in Petersburg. His most famous book is called "Spoon River Anthology." It contains poems or stories that he made up about the people buried in the cemetery. It starts:

Where are Elmer, Herman, Bert, Tom and
  Charley,
The weak of will, the strong of arm, the clown,
  the boozer, the fighter?
All, all, are sleeping on the hill.

Another poet, Vachel Lindsay, was born in Springfield in 1879. He wrote a poem called "Abraham Lincoln Walks at Midnight."

It is portentous, and a thing of state
That here at midnight, in our little town
A mourning figure walks, and will not rest,
Near the old court-house, pacing up and down,

Or by his homestead, or in shadowed yards
He lingers where his children used to play,
Or through the market, on the well-worn
  stones
He stalks until the dawn-stars burn away.

A bronzed, lank man! His suit of ancient black,
A famous high top-hat and plain worn shawl
Make him the quaint great figure that men
  love,
The prairie-lawyer, master of us all.

Illinois College, founded in 1829, is in Jacksonville. It is one of the oldest colleges in the state.

Area Seven

The next area (number 7) of Illinois that we will visit is along the Wabash River and the border with Indiana. This is the area where Lincoln first crossed

314

over into Illinois. This trail, called the Lincoln Heritage Trail, is marked at the beginning by a striking bronze statue of Lincoln walking beside the family's covered wagon. The trail follows the Lincoln family from the point at which they crossed the Wabash near Lawrenceville to the site of their first home near Decatur. It goes on to New Salem and the courthouses where Lincoln earned his **reputation** as a lawyer. It passes the only home he owned and ends at his final resting place.

The fourth Lincoln-Douglas debate was at Charleston. You can visit the debate house. Lincoln's parents are buried in the cemetery here, and they lived here before they died. Lincoln visited them often at Goosenest Prairie farm. Their log cabin home was displayed at the Columbian Exposition in Chicago in 1893, and it mysteriously disappeared. They had to build a replica for the display in the state park. (How could a log cabin disappear? What do you think happened to it?)

Remember Birkbeck and Flower and their English Prairies settlement? Well, it was in this area at Albion. Also there is a large Amish settlement near Arthur and Arcola. These people drive only horse-drawn buggies and no automobiles. They don't use electricity, either, so they have no televisions, radios, refrigerators, or even telephones. They live much as people did a hundred years ago. So, when you are traveling through here, watch out for the horses and buggies!

A German colony was established in 1839 at Teutopolis. In Olney there are white squirrels, but you'll have to watch closely to see one.

You might be interested in the U. S. Grant Hotel in Mattoon. This is where General Grant had his tent when he was getting his troops organized to go into battle. What war was that? Outside the hotel is the original flagpole that stood in front of Grant's tent.

Area Eight

Area Eight is one of the most historic areas in the state. In this area you will see the huge Indian mound at Cahokia. Remember that Cahokia Mound is the largest man-made earthwork on the continent. Cahokia is the oldest town in the state, and the log cabin courthouse is believed to be the oldest structure in the state. The Old Holy Family Church was finished in 1799, and has been restored with the original logs standing **vertically,** as the French built their log buildings.

Pere Marquette State Park near Grafton marks the place where the first white men, Marquette and Joliet, entered Illinois. Remember the Piasa Bird which they saw on the cliffs above the river? Can you see it? Pere Marquette State Park is at the place where the Illinois and Mississippi rivers run together. This is our largest state park.

Alton was the site of the last Lincoln-Douglas debate. There is a state memorial here, too, for Elijah Lovejoy. Remember, he was the **abolitionist** editor who lost his life defending the right to freedom of the press. Alton also had a Confederate prison during the Civil War, and there is a monument to the 1,354 soldiers who died of smallpox during the war.

You can visit the Old State House at Vandalia. Altogether Illinois has had six buildings that served as capitols. The first was at Kaskaskia in the next area. Vandalia had three buildings that served the state, but only one is remaining. The building that you see was used from 1820-1839. Then where did the "Long Nine" want the capital to be moved?

The center of population of the United States is in this area. If you counted all of the people, north, south, east and west, the middle would be near Centralia.

McKendree College, founded in 1828, is located at Lebanon and is also one of the oldest colleges in Illinois. Nearby is the Governor Edward Coles state memorial. He was our second governor.

Salem is the birthplace of William Jennings Bryan. He ran for President as the Democratic Party's candidate three times, but was never elected.

Area Nine

The last area is the southern tip of the state. We are now about 380 miles from the start of our trip. Cairo is at the southernmost tip of the state. It is located where the slate gray Ohio River meets the

317

muddy Mississippi. The town is protected on all sides by **levees.** What two other states can you see from here?

Fort Defiance, established by the North during the Civil War, is at the **confluence** of the two rivers.

Shawneetown was flooded six times, so the whole town was moved to higher ground. The first territorial bank was flooded; it was located on the Ohio River levee. The second bank was completed in 1840 and still stands in Old Shawneetown.

This is the area where salt springs, used by the Indians before white men came, were located. There is an old slave house in this area built by John Hart Crenshaw. He leased the salt springs from the state. The saltmaking industry required a vast amount of labor, so Negro slaves, leased from slaveowners in Kentucky, were brought in to meet this demand.

Cave-in-Rock is a large cave that goes back 108 feet in the Ohio riverbank. This was once the den of bloodthirsty river **pirates** who **preyed** upon the river traffic. One of the earliest robbers to occupy the cave was Samuel Mason, who opened a sort of tavern there in 1797. He and his hostesses developed a technique of serving poison with their **moonshine** and then disposing of the evidence by slitting open the bodies of their victims, filling them with rocks and throwing them in the Ohio River. For nearly four decades (forty years) around the 1800s, river pirates used the cave to **lure** unsuspecting pioneers off the Ohio River, where they were sure to be robbed of their valuables and often their lives. The Harpe Brothers used the cave as headquarters for their outlaw band, and a gang of counterfeiters operated here until 1831. Several years ago, the TV series "Davy Crockett and the River Pirates" was filmed there.

Rosiclare, near the cave, supplied the iron for the gunboats that were constructed at Mound City and used in the Civil War. This area is known as the Old Illinois Iron Furnace.

Shawnee National Forest is nearby. It is the only national forest in the state.

Further down the Ohio River, at Metropolis, is Fort Massac. France established a trading post here in 1701. It was surrendered to the British in 1765 and was burned by a band of Chickasaw Indians. In 1794, George Washington ordered Fort Massac rebuilt. George Rogers Clark entered Illinois near here with his band of Kentucky Long Knives on his way to Kaskaskia to capture the Northwest Territory for America. The third Lincoln-Douglas debate was held at Jonesboro.

You might enjoy a visit to Giant City State Park. It is located in Jackson County. A group of huge blocks of sandstone gives the park its name. They look like city blocks and streets. The park has more than 75 different kinds of trees and over 800 different ferns and flowering plants.

Fluorspar, the official mineral of Illinois, is mined in Hardin County on the Ohio River. Coal is mined in this area, too.

Murphysboro was the scene of a **calamity** on March 18, 1925, when a tornado killed 689 people.

Carbondale is the home of Southern Illinois University. It was also at Carbondale that Memorial Day was begun. In 1867, the people began putting spring flowers on the graves of the war dead. John Logan was responsible for the continuation of the observance on the last Monday in May.

In 1838, the Cherokee Indians were forced from their lands in the Great Smoky Mountains and Georgia to a reservation in Oklahoma. Their trek is called the Trail of Tears Death March. It passed from Golconda to Cape Girardeau, Missouri, touching Dixon Springs, Vienna and Jonesboro. The 15,000 Indians were herded by troops—about 10 percent died due to the cold and snow.

Now we'll go over to Chester and visit the home of Pierre Menard. His home was built in 1802, and he was the first lieutenant governor of Illinois. His home is built in the French colonial style.

And now to Kaskaskia. We will end our tour where Illinois began. The fort at Kaskaskia was located on a **bluff.** In 1778, George Rogers Clark captured Fort Kaskaskia from the British, causing the Illinois country to become a part of Virginia. The town of Kaskaskia was located in the lowlands below the fort. Remember, this was the first capital of Illinois. The Mississippi River cut through the narrow neck of land occupied by the town and washed away its historic buildings. Today the river covers most of the land where the capitol, a two-story, stucco-covered brick residence once stood.

On one of the islands left by the river when it cut its new channel is a memorial building. This houses the "Liberty Bell of the West." This was the bell which rang out proudly when George Rogers Clark captured the town of Kaskaskia. The bell is older than the famous Liberty Bell in Philadelphia. Strangely enough, Kaskaskia Island is now the only part of Illinois to lie west of the Mississippi River. This is true because the boundary of Illinois was fixed before the river changed its **course**, and the old boundary was kept even though the river moved.

Kaskaskia had the first newspaper in the state in 1814. It was called the "Illinois Herald."

You can visit Fort de Chartres at Prairie du Rocher, which was the seat of civil and military government in the Illinois country for fifty years. Fort de Chartres was the last fort in North America to lower the French flag.

So we end our tour at the place where Illinois first became a state. Now you will have to find your own way home.

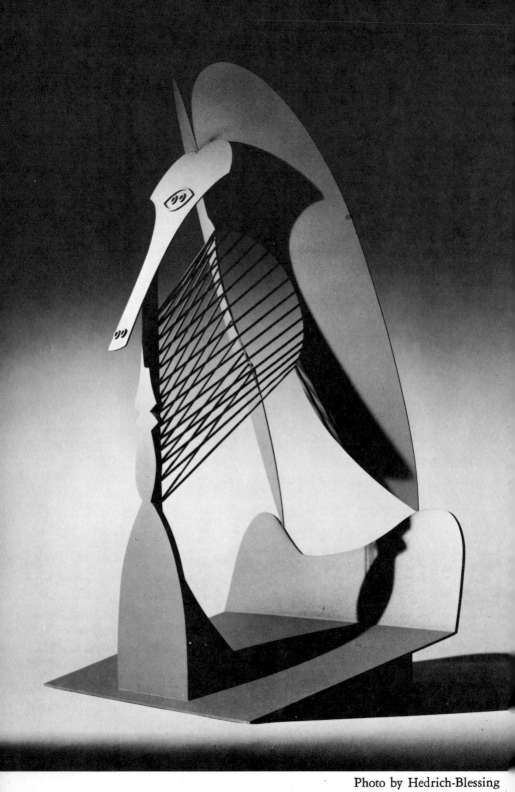

What does this piece of modern art sculpture represent to you? See if you can find out where it is and what artist created it.

Three of the world's five tallest buildings can be found in this skyline view of Chicago. Can you find them and name them?

Buckingham Fountain on Chicago lakefront.

Chicago Convention and Tourism Bureau

Chicago's famous Water Tower, which survived the fire of 1871, contrasted beside the newer John Hancock building.

Chicago Convention and Tourism Bureau

The beautiful, nine-sided Bahai House Of Worship in suburban northshore Chicago area.

Chicago Convention and Tourism Bureau

Farm in the city. A full scale farm yard in Chicago's Lincoln Park.

Chicago's Marina City twin towers.

Chicago Convention and Tourism Bureau

Chicago Museum of Science and Industry

Much of the culture and tradition of the American people can be found in this building.

What do you think they are looking at?

Chicago Museum of Science and Industry

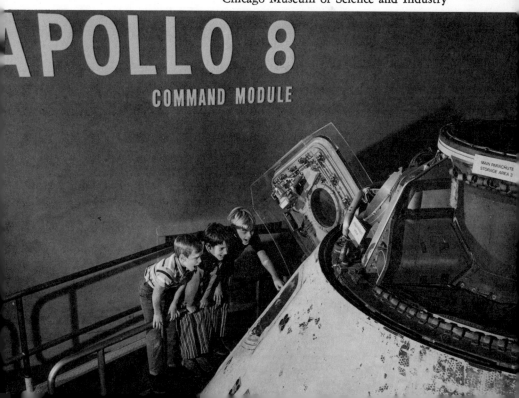

APOLLO 8
COMMAND MODULE

MAIN PARACHUTE
STORAGE AREA 3

Brookfield Zoo, L. LaFrance

Chicago's famous Brookfield Zoo.

Some of the animals in the Brookfield Zoo. What are they?

Brookfield Zoo, L. LaFrance

Popular exhibit at the Field Museum of Natural History is this 75 million year old Gorgosaurus.

The famous Adler Planetarium in Chicago.

The popular painting "American Gothic" by Grant Wood, in the Art Institute of Chicago.

Chicago Convention and Tourism Bureau

These bronze Lions have guarded the entrance to Chicago's famous Art Institute for many years.

Professional sports. The Bears in action.

Chicago Tribune, Sports Department

Professional sports. The Cubs score!

Professional sports. Where is the puck?

Chicago Tribune, Sports Department
Professional sports. Up and in for the Bulls.

Data and Resource Section

PART ONE

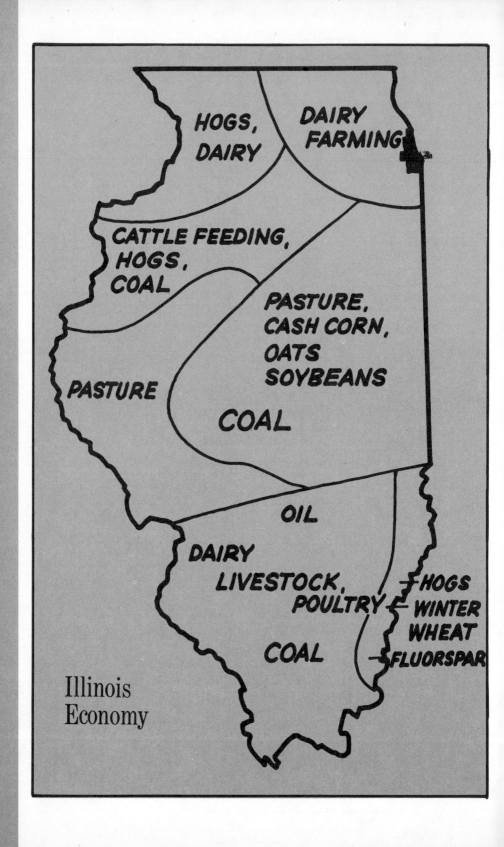

HOGS, DAIRY

DAIRY FARMING

CATTLE FEEDING, HOGS, COAL

PASTURE, CASH CORN, OATS SOYBEANS

COAL

PASTURE

OIL

DAIRY

LIVESTOCK, POULTRY

COAL

HOGS
WINTER WHEAT
FLUORSPAR

Illinois Economy

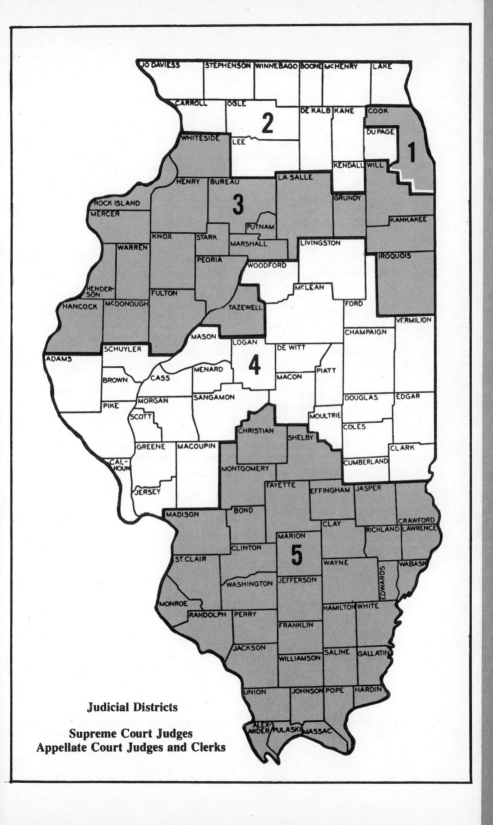

Judicial Districts

Supreme Court Judges
Appellate Court Judges and Clerks

The State Song

An Act Establishing a State Song, by the 54th General Assembly:

Be it enacted by the People of the State of Illinois represented in the General Assembly:

Section 1. The song "Illinois" having words written by C. H. Chamberlain and music composed by Archibald Johnston, is established as the official State Song of Illinois. Words of the song follow:

ILLINOIS

By thy rivers gently flowing, Illinois, Illinois,
O'er thy prairies verdant growing, Illinois, Illinois,
Comes an echo on the breeze,
Rustling through the leafy trees, and its mellow tones are these
      Illinois, Illinois.

From a wilderness of prairies, Illinois, Illinois,
Straight thy way and never varies, Illinois, Illinois,
Till upon the inland sea,
Stands thy great commercial tree, turning all the world to thee,
      Illinois, Illinois,
Turning all the world to thee, Illinois.

When you heard your country calling, Illinois, Illinois
Where the shot and shell were falling, Illinois, Illinois,
When the Southern host withdrew,
Pitting Gray against the Blue, There were none more brave than you,
      Illinois, Illinois,
There were none more brave than you, Illinois.

Not without thy wondrous story, Illinois, Illinois,
Can be writ the nation's glory, Illinois, Illinois,
On the record of thy years,
Abraham Lincoln's name appears, Grant and Logan, and our tears,
      Illinois, Illinois,
Grant and Logan, and our tears, Illinois.

STATISTICAL INFORMATION

Illinois became the 21st state in 1818.

Name: Illinois is the way the French wrote Illini, the Algonquian Indian word meaning men or warriors.

Capital: Springfield.

State Motto: "State sovereignty, national union."

State Slogan: "Land of Lincoln."

State Flower: Native violet.

State Tree: White oak.

State Bird: Cardinal.

State Mineral: Fluorite.

State Song: "Illinois."

Familiar Name: "Prairie State."

Great Seal of Illinois—Authorized March 7, 1867; first used October 26, 1868.

State Flag: Became official July 1, 1970.

Area: 56,400 square miles.

Length: North to south—about 385 miles.

Width: East to west—about 218 miles.

Highest Elevation: 1241 feet above sea level in the northwest corner of the state. (Charles Mound in Jo Daviess County.)

Lowest Elevation: 279 feet above sea level in the southernmost portion of the state. (Cairo, on the Ohio River.)

Average Mean Temperature: 50 degrees.

Summer Mean Temperature: 70 to 80 degrees.

Growing Season—North, 150 days; South, 210 days.

Average Annual Number of Tornadoes—24.

Annual Precipitation: 39 inches.

The Mississippi River forms Illinois' entire west boundary, and the Ohio River the south and southeast boundary, with the Wabash forming the lower east boundary. The principal river is the Illinois, which flows southwestward from Chicago to meet the Mississippi at Alton.

Length of Rivers—Illinois, 273 miles long; Mississippi, 581

miles (Illinois boundary); Ohio, 113 miles (Illinois boundary).

Population: 11,113,976 (1970 census); 10,081,158 (1960 census).

Median Age of State Population: 30.2 years.

Natural Resources: Rich soil, coal, oil, fluorspar, tripoli, stone and peat.

Largest Cities:
Chicago, 3,369,359 (second largest in U. S.).
Rockford, 147, 370.

State University—
University of Illinois (eighth largest in U. S.).
Location: Urbana.
Branch: Chicago.
Total Enrollment: Over 54,000.

Educational Data—

Number of School Districts: 1,849.

Per Pupil Expenditures: $986.

High School Graduates: 136,410 (1972).

State Colleges: 7 with enrollments of over 10,000 (University of Chicago and Loyola in Chicago, Illinois State University in Normal, Northwestern University in Evanston, Northern Illinois University in De Kalb, Southern Illinois University in Carbondale, and Western Illinois University in Macomb).

Community Colleges: 43 (Belleville, Canton, Cartersville, Carthage, Centralia, Champaign, Chicago, Chicago Heights, Cicero, Crystal Lake, Danville, Dixon, East Peoria, Elgin, Evanston, Freeport, Galesburg, Glen Ellyn, Godfrey, Grays Lake, Harrisburg, Ina, Joliet, Kankakee, Lincoln, Mattoon, Moline, Mount Carmel, Olney, Palatine, Palos Hills, River Grove, Rockford, South Holland, Springfield, Sugar Grove, Ullin).

Trade Schools in Illinois, 303.

Transportation Data—

Airports With Commercial Service: 14.

Other Commercial and Municipal Airports: 111.

Airlines Serving Illinois: 26.

(Air Illinois, Allegheny, American, Braniff, Chicago Helicopter, Continental, Ozark, Piedmont, Southern, TWA, United, Eastern, Delta, North Central, Northwest, Air France, Air Jamaica, British Airways, Icelandic, KLM, Lufthansa, Mexicana, Pan Am, SAS, Swissair, and Caribbean.)

Miles of Railroad Track: 23,000 (second in nation).

Railroads Serving Illinois: 27.

(Atchison, Topeka and Santa Fe; Baltimore and Ohio; Chesapeake and Ohio; Burlington Northern*; Chicago and Eastern Illinois; Chicago and Illinois Midland; Chicago and Illinois Western; Chicago and North Western; Chicago Great Western; Chicago, Milwaukee, St. Paul and Pacific; Chicago, Rock Island and Pacific; Elgin, Joliet and Eastern; Erie-Lackawana; Grand Trunk Western; Illinois Central Gulf*; Illinois Terminal; Louisville and Nashville; Missouri-Illinois; Missouri-Kansas-Texas; Missouri-Pacific; Minneapolis, St. Paul and Sault Ste. Marie; Monon; Norfolk and Western; Penn Central*; Soo; Southern; Toledo, Peoria and Western).

Harbor and Barge Terminal Facilities: 8.

(Chicago, East St. Louis, Granite City, Joliet, Peoria, Seneca, Shawneetown, and Waukegan. Chester and Havana being developed.)

Miles of Surfaced State and Local Highways: 16,446.

(U. S. No. 24, 55, 56, 57, 64, 70, 74, 80, 90, 94, 255, 270, 294.)

Miles of Limited-Access Interstate Highways: 1,725.

Major Rivers: 12.

(Big Muddy, Des Plaines, Embarrass, Illinois, Kankakee, Kaskaskia, Mississippi, Ohio, Rock, Sangamon, Spoon, and Wabash.)

Incorporated Villages and Cities: 379 with 2,500 or more population. Under 1,000 population: about 512.

Agricultural Data—

Number of farms in Illinois: 123,565 (1970).

Farm acreage: 29,957,500.

*Amtrak trains run on these railroads.

Average acreage per farm: 242.4+.

Average value per farm: $82,494.

Farms selling products over $10,000 in value: 68,291.

Total cash farm income: $1,278,156,360 in 1972; $2.7 billion in 1970.

Illinois' rank as agricultural state: 2nd (1972).

Livestock and livestock products rank: 7th.
    Receipts total $1,261,491,000.

Principal agricultural products of Illinois: Corn, soybeans, apples, wheat, other small grain crops, hay, hogs, cattle, sheep, poultry.

Illinois Agricultural Products Exported Annually—

Feed grains—298 million bushels.

Beef—552 million pounds.

Pork—546 million pounds.

Eggs—762 million.

Soybeans—85 million bushels.

Percent of agricultural products exported: 40%.

Number of agricultural product processing stations in Illinois, approximate: 2,000.

Honey production, 1970: 4,560,000 pounds.

Beeswax produced annually: 114,000 pounds.

Agriculture and agriculture-related occupations provide one out of every ten jobs in the state.

Illinois provides 10% of the total United States Agricultural products going into international trade.

County Agricultural Fairs Held Annually: 94.

4-H Fairs Held Annually: 102.

Vocational Agricultural Fairs Held Annually: 25.

Livestock and livestock products rank: 7th.
    Cattle slaughter: 7th.
    Meat packing: 7th.
    Fed cattle marketed: 7th.
    Hogs and pigs: 2nd.
    Sheep and lambs: 18th.

Poultry Production:
    Farm chickens raised: 5th.

342

Broilers produced: 9th.
Eggs produced: 5th.
Dairy Production:
Milk produced: 9th.
Creamery butter production: 7th.
American cheese production: 4th.
Ice cream production: 6th.
Total Value Crops: Rank 2nd.

Illinois Soils

Major Soil Groups	Soil Types	Characteristics
Prairie soils, mostly in the central area. Much of this was blown in and is known as loess.	Black soil rich in organic content and in lime.	Holds water well and supports crops well, especially soybeans and corn.
Forest soils, sometimes called "clay pan."	Yellowish to gray with little organic material.	Holds water poorly and is poor in growing plant support.

ILLINOIS AGRICULTURAL PRODUCTION

Basic Grain and Seed Crops—1970 Census Year

Corn—988,740,000 bushels.
Soybeans—212,815,000 bushels.
Wheat—54,000,000 bushels.
Oats—27,720,000 bushels.

Other

Hay—3,373,000 tons.
Barley—765,000 bushels.
Rye—460,000 bushels.
Potatoes—400,000 hundredweight.
Cotton lint—1,000 bales.

Livestock and Poultry on Illinois Farms— 1970 Census Year

Hogs and pigs—11,881,000
Chickens on farms—10,969,000
Cattle on farms—3,245,000
Fed cattle marketed—1,167,000
Sheep on farms—317,000

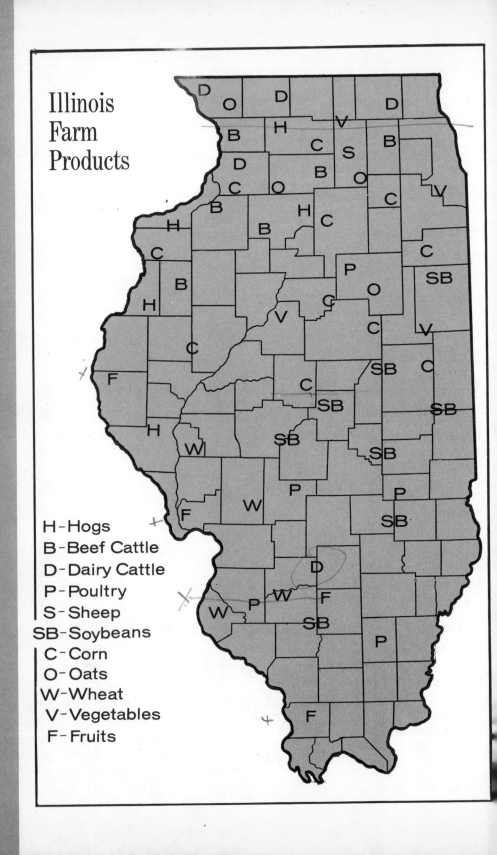

Illinois
Farm
Products

H - Hogs
B - Beef Cattle
D - Dairy Cattle
P - Poultry
S - Sheep
SB - Soybeans
C - Corn
O - Oats
W - Wheat
V - Vegetables
F - Fruits

Production of Milk—1970 Census Year
Milk—2,918,000,000 pounds.

Fruits and Vegetables, average annual production
Apples—2,500,000 bushels.
Peaches—260,000 bushels.
Tomatoes—141,000 tons.

Other products
Eggs—1,905,000,000 number.

MINERAL PRODUCTION
Mineral Production: Rank 8th; $647.5 million (1968).
Fluorspar: 1st.
Peat: 1st.
Stone: 1st; 55,858,000 tons; $80,188,000.
Tripoli: 1st.
Coal: 4th; 62,441,000 tons; $250,685,000.
Petroleum: 5th; 56,391,000 barrels; $173,120,000.
Cement: 9,974,000 barrels; $34,572,000.
Sand-Gravel: 45,609,000 tons; $52,943,000.

Mineral Production in Illinois—1968

Coal—62,441,000 tons $250,685,000
Oil—56,391,000 barrels 173,120,000
Stone—55,858,000 tons 80,188,000
Cement—9,974,000 barrels 34,572,000
Sand-Gravel—45,609,000 tons 52,943,000

TOTAL $591,508,000

Value of Mineral Products in North Central States in Order of Rank

State	Value in $ Millions	Minerals
Illinois	758.3	Coal, petroleum, fluorspar, tripoli, stone, peat
Ohio	701.7	Coal, lime, clays, salt, sand, gravel, petroleum, cement, gypsum, natural gas

Michigan ....670.4 Iron ore, gypsum, peat, iodine, bromine, magnesium, lime, gravel, cement, copper, petroleum, salt

Minnesota ......626.8 Iron ore, sand, gravel, stone, cement

Kansas ....587.6 Helium, petroleum, natural gas, salt

Missouri ....449.7 Lead, barite, lime, cement, coal, iron ore, copper, zinc, asphalt

Indiana ....305.8 Coal, cement, petroleum, limestone, clay, gypsum

Iowa ....136.0 Cement, limestone, sand, gravel, gypsum, coal

North Dakota 99.5 Petroleum, natural gas, natural gas liquids, coal (lignite), salt, peat

Wisconsin ...... 82.6 Zinc, lime, cement, stone, iron ore

Nebraska .... 74.1 Petroleum, cement, lime, pumice, sand, gravel

South Dakota 69.8 Gold, beryllium, silver, petroleum, uranium, cement

(Information from World Almanac of 1974.)

The 15 Leading States in Mineral Production

State	Value in $ Millions	Principal Minerals in Order of Value
Texas	6,808.0	Petroleum, natural gas liquids, cement
Louisiana	5,503.0	Petroleum, natural gas liquids, sulfur
California	1,920.6	Petroleum, natural gas, cement, sand and gravel
W. Va.	1,274.0	Coal, natural gas, stone, sand and gravel
Oklahoma	1,189.5	Petroleum, natural gas, natural gas liquids, stone
Penn.	1,149.1	Coal, cement, sand and gravel
New Mex.	1,046.4	Petroleum, natural gas, copper, potassium salts
Arizona	981.0	Copper, molybdenum, cement, sand and gravel
Kentucky	925.8	Coal, stone, petroleum, natural gas
Illinois	758.3	Coal, petroleum, fluorspar, tripoli, stone, peat

346

Wyoming	717.8	Petroleum, natural gas, sodium carbonate, uranium
Ohio	701.7	Coal, clay, salt, sand and gravel
Michigan	670.4	Iron ore, gypsum, peat, iodine, bromide, magnesium compounds, lime, gravel and sand
Minnesota	626.8	Iron ore, sand and gravel
Kansas	586.8	Petroleum, natural gas, helium, potassium salts

(Source: 1974 World Almanac.)

Petroleum Production

Number of producing oil wells in Illinois: 27,000
Modern refineries in Illinois: 14
Petro-Chemical plants in Illinois: 18
Miles of interstate pipelines: 9,000

MANUFACTURING IN ILLINOIS

Ninety-four percent of all the different types of man-made products listed by the United States government are produced in Illinois' 18,000 factories. This makes Illinois the fourth largest producer of manufactured goods in the United States.

Illinois' yearly income from manufacturing is 17 billion dollars or 37 percent of the state's total income. Industrial profits in Illinois have been climbing rapidly. In 1958, it was $2.9 billion and by 1967 it had reached $4.8 billion. The 1,281,700 factory workers of Illinois take home some 10 million dollars a year.

Chicago and its suburbs in Cook County are the second most important manufacturing region in the United States. The Illinois poet Carl Sandburg called Chicago:

347

Freeport   Rockford   Waukegan

Elgin
Aurora   Cicero   Chicago

Sterling-Rock Falls   Harvey

Rock Island   Joliet   Chicago
Moline   La Salle-Peru   Heights

Kankakee

Galesburg

Peoria
Pekin   Bloomington

Danville

Quincy

Springfield   Decatur

Alton
Granite City
East St. Louis   Belleville

Illinois
Industrial
Counties

● Principal Manufacturing Centers

"Hog Butcher for the World,
Tool Maker, Stacker of Wheat,
Player with Railroads and the Nation's
Freight Handler."

Except for the meat packers, which have moved out, this is still true of Chicago. However, now we must add "electronic equipment" to the "Tool Maker." Also, Chicago is still a leader in the production of other food products besides meat.

The leading steel-producing area of the United States is located on the south side of Chicago. Here steel mills use coal from Pennsylvania and southern Illinois to change iron ore from Minnesota into steel.

Although three quarters of Illinois' industry is located in Cook County, many other Illinois cities are also important industrial centers and most are eagerly seeking to attract new firms. Fifty-five of the nation's five hundred largest firms are located in seventeen Illinois cities.

Joliet is a leader in the production of wallpaper and Rockford is a large producer of hosiery. Owens Illinois, the world's largest maker of glass and glass bottles, is in Alton. Corn Products Company, the largest industry of its kind, is located in Summit, Illinois. The world's largest manufacturer of Ferris wheels, the Eli Bridge Company, is in Jacksonville, Illinois.

Peoria has two of the world's largest firms, a bourbon plant and the Caterpillar Tractor Company.

Caterpillar is the largest employer in Illinois. Besides Peoria, it has plants in Joliet, Aurora and Decatur. Altogether these Caterpillar plants employ a total of 40,000 people.

1967 Census of Manufacturing in Illinois

	Employees	Value Added
Food and Similar Products	120,000	$ 2,512,600,000
Textile Mill Products	5,500	50,500,000
Clothing and Related Products	38,400	293,700,000
Lumber and Wood Products	12,100	112,000,000
Furniture and Fixtures	25,800	280,900,000
Paper and Allied Products	40,900	528,800,000
Printing and Publishing	107,000	1,600,900,000
Chemical and Allied Products	57,400	1,565,800,000
Petroleum and Coal Products	11,100	382,700,000
Rubber and Plastic Products	38,000	474,300,000
Leather and Leather Products	14,000	132,600,000
Stone, Clay and Glass Products	37,900	553,300,000
Primary Metal Industries	108,600	1,654,100,000
Fabricated Metal Products	144,400	1,971,000,000
Machinery, Expert Electrical	223,800	3,415,900,000
Electrical Machinery	211,400	2,445,300,000
Transportation Equipment	45,200	864,200,000
Instruments and Related Products	44,000	656,400,000
Miscellaneous Manufacturing	37,200	394,900,000
TOTAL	1,281,700	$20,004,700,000

(Source: 1697 Census of Manufacturing in Illinois, 1971 Ayers Directory.)

Illinois Firms in the Fortune Directory of the 500 Largest U. S. Industrial Corporations (May 1973)

Rank '72	'71	Company	Headquarters	Sales (Thousands)
15	15	Standard Oil (Ind.)	Chicago	$4,503,372
22	26	International Harvester	Chicago	3,493,274
28	72	Swift	Chicago	3,240,931
29	30	Kraft Co.	Glenview	3,196,789

Rank '72 '71	Company	Head-quarters	Sales (Thousands)
34 40	Caterpillar Tractor	Peoria	2,602,178
42 58	Beatrice Foods	Chicago	2,384,410
68 67	Consolidated Foods	Chicago	1,799,778
90 108	Deere	Moline	1,500,246
91 88	FMC	Chicago	1,497,718
112 110	Borg-Warner	Chicago	1,283,187
122 137	Motorola	Franklin Park	1,163,315
145 160	Illinois Central Industries	Chicago	960,691
176 203	Zenith Radio	Chicago	795,908
180 187	Quaker Oats	Chicago	771,159
185 183	Pullman	Chicago	748,713
188 191	McGraw-Edison	Elgin	737,672
204 191	Archer Daniels Midland	Decatur	675,857
206 217	Northwest Industries	Chicago	665,117
211 220	U. S. Gypsum	Chicago	652,088
214 236	Brunswick	Skokie	633,836
243 227	Container Corp. of America	Chicago	558,783
251 252	Abbott Laboratories	North Chicago	521,818
265 234	Internation Minerals & Chem.	Libertyville	491,169
268 266	National Can	Chicago	475,655
269 261	Universal Oil Products	Des Plaines	473,084
271 319	Gould	Chicago	471,289
274 277	Admiral	Chicago	468,763
282 267	Sunbeam	Chicago	453,209
295 295	Hart Schaffner & Marx	Chicago	423,114
297 263	Ward Foods	Wilmette	414,470
302 291	Libby, McNeil & Libby	Chicago	407,242
308 308	Outboard Marine	Waukegan	394,079
313 310	Interlake	Chicago	387,749
324 317	Morton-Norwich Products	Chicago	367,776
327 336	Bell & Howell	Chicago	365,256
329 398	Allied Mills	Chicago	363,642
335 302	Chicago Bridge & Iron	Oak Brook	354,308
336 320	R. R. Donnelley & Sons	Chicago	353,565
355 384	Square D	Park Ridge	340,267
360 328	A. E. Staley Manufacturing	Decatur	336,085
366 333	American Bakeries	Chicago	331,358
371 334	Gen. Amer. Transportation	Chicago	327,712
375 378	Chemetron	Chicago	319,233

Rank '72 '71	Company	Head- quarters	Sales (Thousands)
379 383	Amsted Industries	Chicago	306,163
380 415	Sundstrand	Rockford	304,130
395 406	Trans Union	Chicago	289,318
408 419	Baxter Laboratories	Morton Grove	278,841
419 434	Signode	Glenview	274,145
422 438	G. D. Searle	Skokie	271,878
423 421	Maremont	Chicago	270,727
428 510	Bluebird	Chicago	264,764
439 439	Bunker Ramo	Oak Brook	251,965
440 451	Roper	Kankakee	251,732
446 454	Masonite	Chicago	248,156
452 491	Cenco	Chicago	239,779
456 450	De Sota	Des Plaines	237,307
463 462	Keystone Consolidated Ind.	Peoria	230,466
482 457	Ceco	Chicago	217,221
484 525	Victor Comptometer	Chicago	215,415
490 480	Gardner-Denver	Quincy	209,650
492 474	Allied Products	Chicago	207,648
494 483	Wm. Wrigley Jr.	Chicago	206,652

Source: Fortune, May 1973.

Illinois Based Firms in the Fortune Directory of the 50 Largest Commercial Banking Companies

Rank '72 '71	Bank	Head- quarters	Assets (Thousands)
9 9	Continental Illinois Corp.	Chicago	$12,468,964
33 32	Harris Trust & Savings Bank ..	Chicago	2,947,301
40 37	Nortrust	Chicago	2,590,099

Source: Fortune, July 1973.

Illinois Based Firms in the Fortune Directory of the 50 Largest Life Insurance Companies

Rank '72 '71	Company	Head- quarters	Assets (Thousands)
21 22	Continental Assurance	Chicago	$1,935,599
26 26	Franklin Life	Springfield	1,411,697
33 35	State Farm Life	Bloomington	1,037,553
48 47	Washington National	Evanston	612,532

Source: Fortune, July 1973.

Illinois Based Firms in the Fortune Directory of the 50 Largest Diversified Financial Companies

Rank '72	'71	Company	Head- quarters	Assets (Thousands)
7	8	CNA Financial	Chicago	$4,362,079
16	14	Household Finance	Chicago	2,677,145
34	30	Walter E. Heller Int'l.	Chicago	1,124,468
45	38	Washington National Corp.	Evanston	675,566

Source: Fortune, July 1973.

Illinois Based Firms in the Fortune Directory of the 50 Largest Retailing Companies

Rank '72	'71	Company	Head- quarters	Sales (Thousands)
1	1	Sears Roebuck	Chicago	$10,991,001
7	7	Marcor	Chicago	3,369,321
10	11	Jewel Companies	Chicago	2,009,294
16	15	National Tea	Chicago	1,613,853
19	17	City Products	Des Plaines	1,477,636
33	32	Walgreen	Chicago	863,334
48	48	Marshall Field	Chicago	492,794

Source: Fortune, July 1973.

Illinois Based Firms in the Fortune Directory of the 50 Largest Transportation Companies

Rank '72	'71	Company	Head- quarters	Operating Revenues (Thousands)
1	2	UAL	Chicago	$1,828,357
12	12	Santa Fe Industries	Chicago	972,841
21	19	Chi. & North Western Trans.	Chicago	370,978
26	24	Chi., Rock Island & Pac. R. R.	Chicago	321,003
27	26	Chicago, Milwaukee	Chicago	319,238
36	34	Allied Van Lines	Broadview	187,347
44	45	Spector Industries	Chicago	125,264

Source: Fortune, July 1973.

Illinois Based Firms in the Fortune Directory of the 50 Largest Utility Companies

Rank '72 '71	Company	Head-quarters	Assets (Thousands)
7 5	Commonwealth Edison	Chicago	$4,336,665
33 31	Peoples Gas	Chicago	1,522,841

Source: Fortune, July 1973.

Sectors of the Illinois Economy

Manufacturing, 26%.
Wholesale and retail, 19%.
Services, 14%.
Government, 13%.
Transportation, Communication and Public Utilities, 8%.
Finance, Insurance and Real Estate, 6%.
Construction, 3%.
Other, 13%.
(Source: The Official Associated Press Almanac, 1973.)

Forest Resources

Today about 10 percent of Illinois, or about four million acres are still covered by forest. Of this, 238,492 acres are in the Shawnee National Forest which stretches across southern Illinois. There is also a smaller forest preserve in Cook County.

The trees in these forests are mainly oak, cottonwood, aspen, elm, maple, sycamore, hickory, red and sap gum, ash, yellow poplar, walnut, beech and basswood. They grow about 400,000 board feet a year. This is more than is harvested, so the forests are gradually expanding into lands unsuitable for farming.

Water Resources

Available water supply from all sources in the state is estimated to be 53 billion gallons per day.

Human Resources

Population of Illinois, 1970: 11,113,976.
Number employed in Illinois, 1971: 4.3 million.
National unemployment average, 1971: 6.1%.
Illinois unemployment average, 1971: 4.6%.

Recreation Resources

State Parks and Conservation Areas 91
State Memorials 25
Camping Areas 64
Park Acreage 93,100
State Forests 4
Number of Lakes and Reservoirs 900

COMMUNICATION FACILITIES IN ILLINOIS

TELEPHONES—
Total in cities over 100,000 in 1973—3,014,026
Total Telephones—5,823,000
Type of Service:
  Business—2,031,000
  Residence—5,312,000
Ownership:
  Bell Companies—84.1%
  Other—15.9%
Telephones per 100 population: 57
Percent of households with telephones: 92%
(Sources: 1973 Statistical Abstract, and Pocket Data Book.)

COMMERCIAL BROADCAST STATIONS (Jan. 1, 1972)
  Total—252
  AM—121
  FM—107
  TV—24

DAILY AND SUNDAY NEWSPAPERS (1971)
  Total Daily—102
  Net paid circulation (Daily)—3,896,311
  Total Sunday—19

Net paid circulation (Sunday)—2,424,148
Total Weekly and Semiweekly Papers—662
Number of Post Offices—1,299
(Sources: Illinois Blue Book 1971-1972, World Almanac
1974, 1971 Ayers Directory.)

STATE INSTITUTIONS

Channahon School Camp
Chicago Program Center
Dixon Springs School Camp
Du Page State Boys' School
Field Services Division
    Family and Youth Counseling Service
Fort Massac School Camp
Giant City Forestry Camp
Hanna City State Boys' School
Illinois Industrial School for Boys
Illinois State Penitentiary
    Illinois State Farm
    Joliet-Stateville Branch
    Menard Branch
    Pontiac Branch
    Vienna Branch
Illinois State Training School for Boys
Illinois State Training School for Girls
Kankakee School Camp
Mississippi Palisades Forestry Camp
New Salem Forestry Camp
Pere Marquette School Camp
Reception and Diagnostic Center
State Reformatory for Women
Valley View School for Boys

TOURISM IN ILLINOIS

By far the largest industry in Illinois is tourism.
In 1966, it reached a peak of two billion dollars. Sixty
percent of this money was spent by fifty-two million
out-of-state visitors.

356

Tourist Accommodations

Resorts: 5
Motels: 250
Hotels and Motor Inns: 112

Fishing Licenses

	1969	1970
Resident	836,169	857,016
Nonresident	36,248	38,502
TOTAL	872,417	895,518

(Source: Department of Conservation Annual Report.)

Hunting Licenses (Small Game)

	1969	1970
Resident	427,404	447,490
Nonresident	7,975	8,596
TOTAL	435,379	456,086

Fisheries

Total Catch (1967 estimate): 7,271,000 lbs.; $776,000 value.
Principal Fish: Catfish, Buffalo Fish, Carp.

THE QUALITY OF LIFE IN ILLINOIS

Economic Growth: Illinois ranks 4th among all states.
Personal Income: Illinois is 3rd in nation, although 24th in land area.
Agricultural Exports: Illinois leads nation.
MDTA (Manpower Development and Training Act) provides training for unemployed and underemployed.
VTA (Vocational Training Act) is similar to above.
230 industrial districts or parks.
All religious denominations throughout Illinois.
Technological Change: Illinois ranks 1st.
Education: Illinois ranks 17th in money spent per pupil.
Health and Welfare: Illinois ranks 23rd in number of physicians per 100,000 population.
Living Conditions: Illinois ranks 4th in number of households.

MISCELLANEOUS

Aircraft, Civil: 5,339

Airports: 433

Banks, total: 1,076
  Assets: $54,633,507,000
  Deposits: $45,431,781,000
  Liabilities: $50,176,133,000
  Loans and Securities: $46,255,796,000
  Reserves: $4,457,334,000

Births:
  1972—175,604
  1971—192,321 (highest in the nation)

Congressional Districts:
  26 in 1940
  25 in 1950
  24 in 1960 and 1970

Crime Rate: 2,483.8 per 100,000 population, 13th highest in the nation

Death Rates:
  1972—108,894
  1971—107,217 (2nd highest in the nation)

Divorce Rate: 1972—43,164 (3rd highest in the nation)

Marriage Rate: 1972—118,087 (2nd highest in the nation)

Motor Vehicles Registered: 5,325,000; rank 6th (Sept. 1970 estimate)

Retail Stores: 89,203; sales, $19,252,390,000

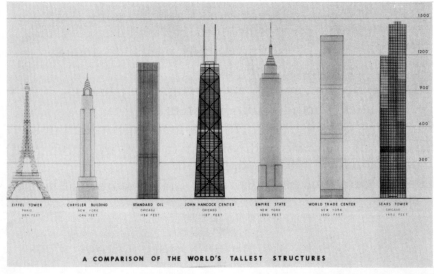

A COMPARISON OF THE WORLD'S TALLEST STRUCTURES

Sears, Roebuck and Company

IMPORTANT BRIDGES

Type	Year	Name	Location	Longest Span (Feet)
Suspension	1935	Memorial Twin	Mississippi R.	710
Cantilever	1932	Savanna-Sabvia	Mississippi R.	1,160
Cantilever	1918	McArthur	Mississippi R.	1,000
Cantilever	1938	Cairo	Ohio R.	800
Cantilever	1930	Cairo	Mississippi R.	800
Cantilever	1905	Thebes	Mississippi R.	672
Cantilever	1942	Chester	Mississippi R.	671
Steel Truss	1910	McKinley, St. Louis	Mississippi R.	500
Continuous Truss	1939	Lyons-Fulton*	Mississippi R.	1,340
Continuous Truss	1929	Chain of Rocks	Mississippi R.	699
Continuous Truss	1932	Mount Carmel	Wabash R.	675
Continuous Truss	1946	Chester	Mississippi R.	670
Continuous Truss	1930	Quincy	Mississippi R.	628
Continuous Truss	1938	Meredosia	Illinois R.	567
Continuous Truss	1936	Mark Twain Mem.	Hannibal, Mo.	562
Continuous Plate	1965	New Chain of Rocks**	Mississippi R.	2,755
Continuous Plate	1965	Rock Island	Mississippi R.	1,136
Steel Arch	1847	Eads, St. Louis	Mississippi R.	520
Vertical Lift	1936	Hardin	Illinois R.	309
Bascule	1926	At. & S.F. R.R.	Mississippi R.	529

*Second longest Continuous Truss bridge in the United States.
**Longest Continuous Plate bridge in the United States.

PARK AND RECREATION AREAS

Name	Location	Facilities
STATE PARKS		
Apple River Canyon	Near Apple River	C, P, R, DW, T, HI
Argyle Lake	Near Colchester	C, E, P, R, DW, T, HI
Baldwin Lake	Baldwin	P, B, F
Beall Woods	Rochester	P, B, F, M
Beaver Dam	Macoupin Sta.	C, E, P, R, DW, T, HI, B, F
Black Hawk	Rock Island	C, E, P, R, DW, T, HI
Buffalo Rock	Near Naplate	P, R, DW, T, HI, F
Cahokia Mounds	BR40, State Park Place	C, E, P, DW, T, HI
Castle Rock	R2 Oregon	P
Cave-in-Rock	S. of Shawneetown on Ill. 1	C, E, P, R, DW, T, HI, B, F
Chain O'Lakes	Near Channel Lake on Ill. 173	C, E, P, R, DW, T, HI, B, F, HU, RP
Delabar	Near Oguauka	C, E, P, R, DW, T, HI, B
Dixon Springs	Dixon Springs on Ill. 146	C, P, DW, T, HI, S, F
Douglas County	Near Oakland on Ill. 133	P, T, HI, B, F
Eldon Hazlett	Near Carlyle on U.S. 50	C, P, DW, T, HI, B, F, HU
Ferne Clyffe	Goreville on Ill. 37	C, E, P, DW, T, HI, F
Fort Chartres	Nr. Prairie du Rocher on Ill. 155	P, R, DW, T, M
Fort Creve Coeur	Creve Coeur on U.S. 66	P, DW, T
Fort Defiance	At Cairo	P, DW, T, B, F
Fort Kaskaskia	Near Chester	P, DW, T, B, F
Fort Massac	Metropolis on U.S. 45	C, P, DW, T, HI, B, F, M
Fox Ridge	Near Diona on Ill. 130	C, P, R, DW, T, HI, B, F
Frank Hotten	In E. St. Louis	C, P, DW, T, HI, B, F
Gebhard Woods	Morris on Ill. 47	P, DW, T, HI, F
Grant City	S. of Carbondale on U.S. 51	C, E, CB, P, R, DW, T, HI, B, F, M
Goose Lake Prairie	Morris on Ill. 47	Under Development
Henderson County, Gladstone Lake	Gladstone on U.S. 40	C, P, DW, T, HI, B, F
Hennepin Canal	Buda on Ill. 88	C, P, T, HI, B, F
Horseshoe Lake	Olive Branch on Ill. 3	C, P, R, DW, T, HI, B, F, HU
Illini	Marseilles on U.S. 6	C, E, P, R, DW, T, HI, B, F, RP
Illinois Beach	N. of Waukegan on Sheridan Rd.	C, E, L, P, R, DW, T, HI, S, B, F, RP, M
Johnson Sauk Trail	Near Kewanee on Ill. 78	C, E, P, R, DW, T, HI, S, B, F, RP
Jubilee College	Near Brimfield, U.S. 74	C, P, R, DW, T, HI
Kankakee River	Kankakee, Ill. 113	C, E, P, R, DW, T, HI, B, F, HU, RP
Kickapoo	Danville, U.S. 74	C, P, R, DW, T, HI, B, F, RP, M
Lake Le-Aqua-Na	Near Lena, Ill. 73	C, E, P, R, DW, T, HI, B, F
Lake Murphysboro	Murphysboro, Ill. 13	C, E, P, R, DW, T, HI, B, F
Lake Shelbyville (E.)	Windsor, Ill. 32	C, P, HI, T, B, F, HU
Lake Shelbyville (W.)	Shelbyville, Ill. 16	C, P, T, HI, B, F, HU
Lawrence, C. Warren	Lincolnwood, Touhy Ave.	P, DW, T
Lewis & Clark	N. of Granite City, Ill. 3	P, T
Lincoln Log Cabin	S. of Charleston, Ill. 130	C, P, DW, T, HI, RP
Lincoln's New Salem	N.W. of Springfield, Ill. 97	C, E, P, R, DW, T, HI, F, RP, M
Linc. Trail Homestead	W. of Decatur off U.S. 36	C, P, DW, T, HI, F, RP
Lincoln Trail	S. of Marshall off Ill. 1	C, E, P, R, DW, T, HI, B, F, RP
Lowden Memorial	Oregon, Ill. 2	C, E, P, R, DW, T, HI, B, F, RP
Mathiessen	Oglesby, Ill. 51	P, R, DW, T, HI, F
McHenry Dam	Crystal Lake, U.S. 14	P, R, DW, T, B, F
McLean Co., Dawson Lake	Near LeRoy, U.S. 150	C, E, P, R, DW, T, HI, B, F, HU, RP
Mississippi Palisades	Savanna, Ill. 84	C, E, P, R, DW, T, HI, F, B, RP, M
Montebello	Hamilton, Ill. 96	C, P, T, B, F
Morrison-Rockwood-Carleton	Lake Morrison, U.S. 30	C, P, T, HI, B, F
Nauvoo-Horton Lake	Nauvoo, Ill. 96	C, E, P, R, DW, T, B, HI, F, RP, M

Name	Location	Facilities
Pere Marquette	Grafton, Ill. 100	C, E, CB, L, P, R, DW, T, HI, B, F, RP, M
Prophetstown	Prophetstown, Ill. 78	C, E, P, DW, T, HI, B, F
Pyramid	Du Quoin, Ill. 152	C, P, T, HI, B, F, HU
Railsplitter	Broadwell, U.S. 36	P
Ramsey Lake	Ramsey, U.S. 51	C, E, P, R, DW, T, B, F, RP
Randolph County	Chester, Ill. 5	C, P, R, T, HI, B, F, HU
Red Hills	Near Lawrenceville, U.S. 50	C, E, P, R, DW, T, HI, B, F, HU, RP
Rend Lake	Near Benton, U.S. 57	P, B, F, HU
Rock Cut-Pierce Lake	Near Belvidere, BR 20	C, E, P, R, DW, T, HI, B, F, RP, M
Saline Co.-Glen O. Jones Lake	Near Harrisburg, U.S. 45	C, P, R, DW, T, HI, B, F, HU
Sam Dale Lake	Near Xenia, U.S. 50	C, E, P, R, DW, T, HI, B, F, HU
Sam Parr	Newton, Ill. 33	P, T, HI, B, HU
Sangchris Lake	Near Pawnee, Ill. 104	C, PT, HI, B
Siloam Springs	Near Mt. Sterling, U.S. 24	C, E, P, R, DW, T, HI, B, F
Silver Springs	Plano, U.S. 34	P, T, HI, B, F, M
South Shore	Sandoval, U.S. 50	C, P, DW, T, HI, B, F
Spitler Woods	Near Decatur, U.S. 36	C, P, DW, T, HI, B, F
Spring Lake	Near Banner, U.S. 24	C, E, P, R, DW, T, HI, B, F, HU, RP
Starved Rock	Near Ottawa, U.S. 80	C, CB, L, P, R, DW, T, HI, B, F, RP, M
Stephen A. Forbes	Near Salem, U.S. 50	C, P, DW, T, HI, B, F, HU
Washington County	Nashville, Ill. 127	C, E, P, R, DW, T, HI, B, F, HU
Weinberg-King	Brooklyn, Ill. 101	P
Weldon Springs	Clinton, Ill. 10	C, E, P, R, DW, T, H, B, F, RP
White Pines	Mt. Morris, Ill. 64	C, CB, L, P, R, DW, T, HI, F, RP
Wm. G. Stratton	Morris, Ill. 47	P, DW, T, HI, B, F

STATE CONSERVATION AREAS

Name	Location	Facilities
Anderson Lake	Marbletown, Ill. 100	C, E, P, R, DW, T, HI, F, B HU
Carlyle Lake	Carlyle, U.S. 50	C, P, HI, B, F, HU
Chain O'Lakes	Channel Lake, Ill. 173	C, E, P, R, DW, T, HI, C, F, HU
Des Plaines	Elwood, U.S. 66	HU
Iroquois	Near Kankakee, Ill. 1	DW, T, HU
Lake Shelbyville	Shelbyville, Ill. 128	P, B, F, HU
Lee Co. (Green River)	Near Ohio, Ill. 26	DW, T, HU
Marshall County	Sparland, Ill. 29	C, E, P, R, DW, T, B, F, HU
Mermet Lake	Mermet, U.S. 45	P, DW, T, B, F, HU
Piasa Creek	Near Alton, Ill. 100	P, R, DW, T, B, F
Rend Lake	Rend Lake, U.S. 57	P, B, F, HU
Rice Lake	Banner, U.S. 24	P, DW, T, B, F, HU
Rock River	Dixon, Ill. 2	Undeveloped
Sanganois	Browning, Ill. 100	DW, T, B, F, HU
Union County	Reynoldsville, Ill.3	DW, T, F, HU
Wm. H. Power— Wolf Lake	Chicago, U.S. 90	P, DW, T, HI, B, F
Woodford County	Near Peoria, Ill. 26	C, E, P, R, DW, T, B, F, HU

STATE FORESTS

Name	Location	Facilities
Big River (Henderson)	Near Bald Bluff, Ill. 94	C, P, HI, F
Sand Ridge (Mason)	Havana, U.S. 136	C, P, T, HI, F
Hidden Springs (Shelby)	Near Shelbyville, Ill. 128	C, P, T, F
Trail of Tears (Union)	Jonesboro, Ill. 127	P, T, F

SHAWNEE NATIONAL FOREST

Name	Location	Facilities
Bell Smith Springs	Near Glendale, Ill. 145	C, P, T, HI, B, F
Garden of the Gods	Herod, Ill. 34	C, P, T, HI, B, F
Lake Glendale	Dixon Springs, Ill. 145	C, PR, DW, T, HI, S, B, F
Land of Egypt	New Burnside, U.S. 45	C, P, DW, T, F
Ohio River	Golconda, Ill. 146	C, P, DW, T, F

361

Name	Location	Facilities
Pine Hills	Alto Pass, Ill. 127	C, P, DW, T, HI
Pound Hollow	Near Herod, Ill. 34	C, P, DW, T, HI, HU
Tower Rock	Elizabethtown, Ill. 146	C, P, DW, T, HI, F, HU
Turkey Bayou	Near Elizabethtown, Ill. 146	C, P, DW, T, B, F, HU

Facilities: B—Boating, C—Camping, CB—Cabins, DW—Drinking Water, E—Electricity, F—Fishing, HI—Hiking, HU—Hunting, L—Lodge or Hotel, M—Museum or Interpretive Programs, P—Picnic, R—Refreshments, RP—Recreation Programs (some summer only), S—Swimming, T—Toilets.

STATE MEMORIALS

A. Lincoln Home	Springfield
A. Lincoln Tomb	Springfield
Bishop Hill	N. of U.S. 34
Bryant Cottage	Bement on Ill. 105
Douglas Tomb	Chicago East End 35th St.
Gov. Bond Monument	Chester on Ill. 3, Cemetery
Gov. Duncan House (DAR)	Jacksonville, U.S. 36
Jubilee College	N.W. of Peoria, N. of U.S. 150
Kaskaskia	Near Chester
Linc. Trail Monument	E. of Lawrenceville, U.S. 50
Lovejoy Monument	Alton off Ill. 140
Old State Capitol	Springfield
Shawneetown	On Ill. 13
U.S. Grant Home— Old Market House	Galena
Vandalia State House	Vandalia on Alternate U.S. 40

FEDERAL AREAS

Chicago Portage	Chicago, between Chicago R. and Des Plaines R.
Lincoln Home	Springfield, U.S. 36
Shawnee Natl. Forest	Southern Illinois

PART TWO

RESOURCE REFERENCES

Clarence Alvord, *Illinois in the Eighteenth Century.*
Arthur C. Boggess, *The Settlement of Illinois, 1778-1830.*
Solon Justin Buck, *Illinois in 1818.*
*Allan Carpenter, *Illinois, Land of Lincoln.*
Gov. Thomas Ford, *A History of Illinois, 1818 to 1847.*
Neil F. Garvey, *The Government and Administration of Illinois.*
Frank J. Heinl, *Newspapers and Periodicals in the Lincoln-Douglas Country, 1831-1832.*
Robert P. Howard, *Illinois: A History of the Prairie State.*
*Michael J. Howlett, *Handbook of Illinois Government.*
Illinois Blue Book.
Randall Parrish, *Historic Illinois.*
Theodore C. Pease, *The Story of Illinois.*
J. Nick Perrin, *Perrin's History of Illinois.*
U. S. Library of Congress, *Illinois, the Sesquicentennial of Statehood.*
*Carl and Rosalie Frazier, *The Lincoln Country in Pictures.*
*Of special interest to young readers.

Illinois State Historical Library

Emile Vallet, *An Icarian Communist in Nauvoo.*
Anthony F. C. Wallace, *Prelude to Disaster: The Course of Indian-White Relations Which Led to the Black Hawk War of 1832.*

Illinois State Historical Society Publications:
James N. Adams, *Illinois Place Names.*
John W. Allen, *Legends and Lore of Southern Illinois.*
Helen M. Cavanagh, *Funk of Funk's Grove.*
George Rogers Clark and the Revolution in Illinois.
Guide to Pierre Menard Collection.
Illinois in World War II.
Illinois State Historical Society, History, Activities . . .
Lincoln's Inner Circle.
Mr. Lincoln Opens His Mail.
Lloyd Ostendorf, *The Photographs of Mary Todd Lincoln.*
Virgil J. Vogel, *Indian Place Names in Illinois.*
Clyde G. Walton, *An Illinois Gold Hunter in the Black Hills.*

A Chicago Book List

Carlson, Evelyn F. *A Great City and State*. Chicago: King Co., 1947. This book clearly defines the forces responsible for Chicago's development and shows the ways in which Chicago is important to Illinois, and Illinois to Chicago.

Cromie, Robert. *The Great Chicago Fire*. New York: McGraw-Hill Book Co., Inc., 1958. The story of the Chicago fire from its beginning in Mrs. O'Leary's cowshed to the awards for bravery in fighting the fire.

Dedmon, Emmett. *Fabulous Chicago*. New York: Random House, 1953. A social history of Chicago from 1820 to 1953, written by a Chicago newspaperman.

Grant, Bruce. *Fight for a City: The Story of the Union League Club of Chicago and Its Times, 1880-1955*. Chicago: Rand McNally & Co., 1955. An oath taken by eleven men in 1862 becomes the creed of Union League members as they work for good.

Hayes, Dorsha. *Chicago, Crossroads of American Enterprise*. New York: Julian Messner, Inc., 1944. For young people whose increased sense of social responsibility should help them in building a greater city than now stands at the foot of Lake Michigan.

Jensen, George Peter. *Historic Chicago Sites*. Chicago: Excella Press for Creative Enterprises, 1953. Chicago's development is colorfully traced through the stories surrounding some sixty bronze markers of historical places and buildings.

Kogan, Herman, and Wendt, Lloyd. *Lords of the Levee: The Story of Bathhouse John and Hinky Dink*. New York: Bobbs-Merrill Co., 1943. An entertaining account of the lives of two notorious characters and their influence on Chicago's society.

———— *Chicago: A Pictorial History*. New York: E. P. Dutton & Co., 1958. The history of Chicago is told through the use of more than four hundred illustrations.

Lewis, Lloyd. *John S. Wright, Prophet of the Prairies*. Chicago: Prairie Farmer Publishing Co., 1941. The story of a man, relatively forgotten by his city, although he was the founder of her public school system, and responsible for the planning of her lovely parks.

Pierce, Bessie L. *A History of Chicago.* New York: Alfred A. Knopf, Inc., 1937. A scholarly three-volume history for older students.

Poole, Ernest. *Giants Gone: Men Who Made Chicago.* New York: Whittlesey House, McGraw-Hill Book Co., Inc., 1943. The story of men who were the pioneers of a great city, men whose spirit and generosity, as well as ruthlessness, created the Chicago of today.

Where to Write for Information About Illinois

For "Calendar of Events," "Camping Guide," or "Illinois Tour Guide" write to:
> Division of Tourism
> Illinois Dept. of Business and Economic Development
> 222 South College
> Springfield, Ill. 62706

For information on Black Hawk Hills area write to:
> Black Hawk Hills
> Tourism Council
> 815 East State Street
> Rockford, Ill. 61101

For information on early Illinois history write to:
> Step Into Illinois History
> Box 328
> Petersburg, Ill. 62675

For information on the Lincoln area write to:
> Greater Lincoln Area
> Chamber of Commerce
> Box 418
> Lincoln, Ill. 62656

For information on Southwestern Illinois area write to:
> Southwestern Illinois Expeditionland
> Box 286
> Belleville, Ill. 62222

For information on Western Illinois write to:
> Scenic Western Illinois
> Tourism Council
> 901 North Tenth
> Quincy, Ill. 62301

For information on Central Illinois write to:
> Region Four Tourism Council

1701 Third Avenue
Moline, Ill. 61265

For information on Central and Eastern Illinois write to:
Heartland Tourism Council
Box 1051
Champaign, Ill. 61820

For information on Northeastern Illinois write to:
Region One Tourism Council
Box 215
Ingleside, Ill. 60041

For information on Chicago area write to:
Chicago Convention and Tourism Bureau
332 South Michigan Avenue
Chicago, Ill. 60604

Other Sources of Information

Illinois Central Gulf Railroad
Mr. Don Heimburger, Public Relations Dept.
General Office
233 North Michigan Ave.
Chicago, Illinois 60605

Illinois Commerce Commission
Office of Public Information
527 East Capitol
Springfield, Illinois 62701

Illinois Department of Economic Development
Mr. Richard J. Smith, Public Relations Executive
222 South College
Springfield, Illinois 62704

Illinois Information Service
Public Relations Department
201 West Monroe St.
Springfield, Illinois 62706

Illinois State Historical Society
Mr. William K. Alderfer, State Historian
Old State Capitol
Springfield, Illinois 62706

PART THREE

ORIGIN OF COUNTY NAMES

Adams—John Quincy Adams, sixth president of the United States.

Alexander—William M. Alexander, early settler of the district and state representative in the 2nd and 3rd General Assemblies.

Bond—Governor Shadrach Bond, first governor of Illinois.

Boone—Daniel Boone, pioneer hunter, explorer and Indian fighter.

Brown—General Jacob Brown, soldier in War of 1812.

Bureau—Pierre de Bureo, French trader with the Indians.

Calhoun—John C. Calhoun, Southern statesman and U. S. vice president under Monroe.

Carroll—Charles Carroll of Carrollton, a signer of the Declaration of Independence.

Cass—General Lewis Cass, secretary of war under President Jackson and secretary of state under President Buchanan.

Champaign—Named for a county in Ohio.

Christian—Named for a county in Kentucky.

Clark—George Rogers Clark, soldier of the Revolution, captor of Fort Vincennes and Kaskaskia.

Clay—Henry Clay, famed politician and author of the "Missouri Compromise."

Clinton—De Witt Clinton, mayor of the city and governor of the state of New York, promoter of the Erie Canal.

Coles—Governor Edward Coles, supporter of antislavery movement.

Cook—Daniel P. Cook, pioneer lawyer, first attorney general of Illinois and member of Congress from 1819 to 1827.

Crawford—William H. Crawford, prominent Georgia U. S. senator, candidate for president in 1824.

Cumberland—Named for Cumberland Road.

De Kalb—Johann De Kalb, German baron who fought in the Revolution; killed in 1790.

De Witt—Named for De Witt Clinton (see Clinton).

Douglas—Stephen A. Douglas, U. S. senator from Illinois, 1847 to 1861.

Du Page—Named for Du Page River.

Edgar—John Edgar, pioneer merchant and politician.

Edwards—Governor Ninian Edwards.

Effingham—Lord Edward Effingham, who resigned his post in the British Army rather than fight the colonies in 1775.

Fayette—Marquis de Lafayette, Frenchman who aided colonists in Revolutionary War.

Ford—Governor Thomas Ford.

Franklin—Benjamin Franklin, famed statesman, U. S. ambassador to France during Revolution.

Fulton—Robert Fulton, first successful builder of steamboats on American water.

Gallatin—Albert Gallatin, financier and member of Congress from Pennsylvania.

Greene—General Nathaniel Greene, commander in southern colonies during Revolution.

Grundy—Felix Grundy, U. S. senator from Tennessee and attorney general of the U. S.

Hamilton — Alexander Hamilton, Revolutionary soldier and first secretary of treasury, 1789 to 1795.

Hancock—John Hancock, Revolutionary soldier and first signer of Declaration of Independence.

Hardin—Named for a county in Kentucky.

Henderson—Named for Henderson River.

Henry—Patrick Henry, famed orator, Revolutionary soldier and governor of Virginia.

Iroquois—Named after Indian tribe.

Jackson—Andrew Jackson, seventh president of the U. S.

Jasper — Sgt. William Jasper, Revolutionary hero at Charleston and Savannah.

Jefferson—Thomas Jefferson, wrote the Declaration of Independence, third president of the U. S.

Jersey—Named for New Jersey.

Jo Daviess—Joseph Hamilton Daviess, prominent Kentucky lawyer and soldier slain at Battle of Tippecanoe in 1811.

Johnson—Colonel Richard M. Johnson, reputed to have killed Indian Chief Tecumseh; U. S. vice president 1837-1841.

Kane—Senator Elias K. Kane, first secretary of state of Illinois.

Kankakee—Named after Indian tribe.

Kendall—Amos Kendall, postmaster general under President Jackson, and partner of S. B. Morse, inventor of the telegraph.

Knox—General Henry Knox, Revolutionary hero and Washington's secretary of war.

Lake—Named for Lake Michigan.

La Salle—Sieur de La Salle, French explorer of America.

Lawrence—Captain James Lawrence, commander of U. S. Chesapeake and killed in naval battle in 1812.

Lee—Richard Henry Lee, orator and statesman of the Revolution.

Livingston—Edward Livingston, secretary of state under President Jackson.

Logan—Dr. John Logan, pioneer physician and father of General John A. Logan.

Macon—Nathaniel Macon, Revolutionary soldier and later U. S. senator.

Macoupin—Named after Indian name.

Madison—James Madison, fourth president of the United States.

Marion—General Francis Marion, distinguished soldier in Carolinas during the Revolution.

Marshall—John Marshall, famous as chief justice of the U. S. Supreme Court.

Mason—Named for a county in Kentucky.

Massac—Named for Fort Massac.

McDonough—Commodore Thomas McDonough, who defeated the British on Lake Champlain in 1814.

McHenry—General William McHenry, fought in War of 1812 and Black Hawk War, also served in several early General Assemblies.

McLean—John McLean, first representative in Congress for Illinois in 1818 and U. S. senator 1824 to 1825.

Menard—Pierre Menard, first lieutenant governor in Illinois.

Mercer—General Hugh Mercer, killed in Battle of Princeton during Revolution.

Monroe—James Monroe, fifth president of the United States.

Montgomery—General Richard Montgomery, Revolutionary soldier of Irish birth, killed at Quebec in 1775.

Morgan—General Daniel Morgan, who earned distinction during Revolution at Quebec and Saratoga.

Moultrie—General William Moultrie, successful defender of Fort Moultrie at Charleston during the Revolution.

Ogle—Lieutenant Joseph Ogle, member of Territorial Militia.

Peoria—Named after Indian name.

Perry—Commodore Oliver H. Perry, who won distinction in the Battle of Lake Erie in 1813.

Piatt—Benjamin Piatt, attorney general of the Illinois Territory, 1810 to 1813.

Pike—Zebulon M. Pike, general in the war of 1812.

Pope—Nathaniel Pope, first territorial secretary of state from 1809 to 1816.

Pulaski—Count Casimir Pulaski, Polish hero killed in the attack on Savannah in 1779.

Putnam—General Israel Putnam, Revolutionary soldier.

Randolph—Edmund Randolph, soldier in the Revolution and secretary of state and attorney general under Washington.

Richland—Named for a county in Ohio.

Rock Island—Named for island in Rock River.

Saline—Named for Saline Creek.

Sangamon—Named after Indian name.

Schuyler—General Philip Schuyler, soldier in Revolution and later U. S. senator from New York.

Scott—Named after a county in Kentucky.

Shelby—Isaac Shelby, soldier in the Revolution, Indian Wars and War of 1812; governor of Kentucky, 1762-1796.

Stark—General John Stark, Revolutionary soldier who won fame at Bunker Hill, Trenton, Princeton and Bennington.

St. Clair—General Arthur St. Clair, after Revolution, was commander in chief of U. S. Army and governor of U. S. territory northwest of the Ohio.

Stephenson—Colonel Benjamin Stephenson, adjutant general of Illinois Territory 1813-1814.

Tazewell—Lyttelton W. Tazewell, member of Congress 1800-1802, member commission on purchase of Florida, member U. S. Senate 1824-1833, governor of Virginia in 1834.

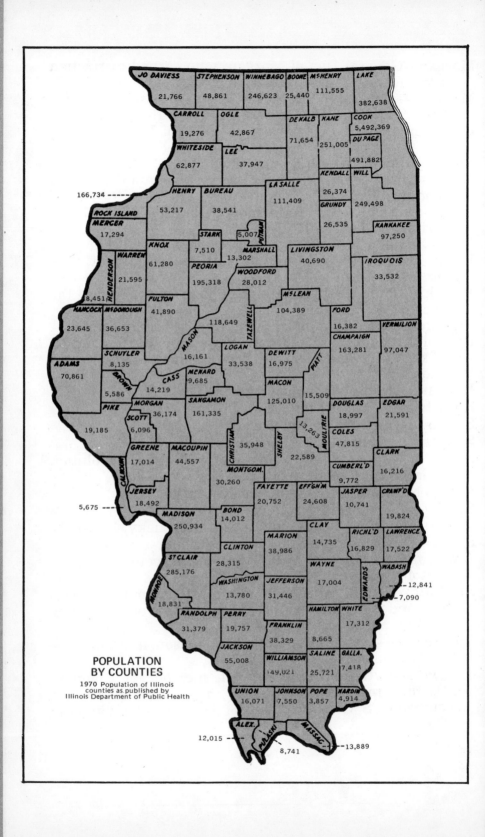

POPULATION
BY COUNTIES

1970 Population of Illinois
counties as published by
Illinois Department of Public Health

JO DAVIESS 21,766
STEPHENSON 48,861
WINNEBAGO 246,623
BOONE 25,440
McHENRY 111,555
LAKE 382,638
CARROLL 19,276
OGLE 42,867
DEKALB 71,654
KANE 251,005
COOK 5,492,369
DU PAGE 491,882
WHITESIDE 62,877
LEE 37,947
KENDALL 26,374
WILL 249,498
166,734
HENRY 53,217
BUREAU 38,541
LA SALLE 111,409
GRUNDY 26,535
KANKAKEE 97,250
ROCK ISLAND
MERCER 17,294
STARK 7,510
PUTNAM 5,007
MARSHALL 13,302
LIVINGSTON 40,690
IROQUOIS 33,532
KNOX 61,280
WARREN 21,595
HENDERSON 8,451
PEORIA 195,318
WOODFORD 28,012
McLEAN 104,389
FORD 16,382
VERMILION 97,047
HANCOCK 23,645
McDONOUGH 36,653
FULTON 41,890
TAZEWELL 118,649
MASON 16,161
LOGAN 33,538
DEWITT 16,975
CHAMPAIGN 163,281
SCHUYLER 8,135
ADAMS 70,861
BROWN 5,586
CASS 14,219
MENARD 9,685
MACON 125,010
PIATT 15,509
DOUGLAS 18,997
EDGAR 21,591
PIKE 19,185
MORGAN 36,174
SCOTT 6,096
SANGAMON 161,335
MOULTRIE 13,263
COLES 47,815
CLARK 16,216
GREENE 17,014
MACOUPIN 44,557
CHRISTIAN 35,948
SHELBY 22,589
CUMBERL'D 9,772
JERSEY 18,492
MONTGOM. 30,260
FAYETTE 20,752
EFF'GH'M 24,608
JASPER 10,741
CRAWF'D 19,824
5,675
MADISON 250,934
BOND 14,012
CLAY 14,735
RICHL'D 16,829
LAWRENCE 17,522
MARION 38,986
CLINTON 28,315
WAYNE 17,004
EDWARDS
WABASH 12,841
7,090
ST CLAIR 285,176
WASHINGTON 13,780
JEFFERSON 31,446
MONROE 18,831
RANDOLPH 31,379
PERRY 19,757
FRANKLIN 38,329
HAMILTON 8,665
WHITE 17,312
JACKSON 55,008
WILLIAMSON 49,021
SALINE 25,721
GALLA. 7,418
UNION 16,071
JOHNSON 7,550
POPE 3,857
HARDIN 4,914
ALEX. 12,015
PULASKI 8,741
MASSAC 13,889

Union—Named for union meeting of Dunkards and Baptists.

Vermilion—Named for Vermilion River.

Wabash—Named after Indian name.

Warren—General Joseph Warren, pioneer physician and soldier, killed at Bunker Hill.

Washington—Named for George Washington.

Wayne—General Anthony Wayne, Revolutionary commander and Indian fighter.

White—Leonard White, member of Constitutional Convention of 1818.

Whiteside—Samuel Whiteside, representative in first General Assembly and brigadier general in Black Hawk War.

Will—Conrad Will, member of the Constitutional Convention of 1818 and member of first to ninth General Assemblies.

Williamson—Named after county in Tennessee.

Winnebago—Named after Indian name.

Woodford—Named after county in Kentucky.

County Population

County	1960	1970	County	1960	1970
Adams	68,467	70,861	Edwards	7,940	7,090
Alexander	16,061	12,015	Effingham	23,107	24,608
Bond	14,060	14,042	Fayette	21,946	20,752
Boone	20,326	25,440	Ford	16,606	16,382
Brown	6,210	5,586	Franklin	39,281	38,329
Bureau	37,594	38,541	Fulton	41,954	41,890
Calhoun	5,933	5,675	Gallatin	7,638	7,418
Carroll	19,507	19,276	Greene	17,460	17,014
Cass	14,539	14,219	Grundy	22,350	26,535
Champaign	132,436	163,281	Hamilton	10,010	8,665
Christian	37,207	35,948	Hancock	24,574	23,645
Clark	16,546	16,216	Hardin	5,879	4,914
Clay	15,815	14,735	Henderson	8,237	8,451
Clinton	24,029	28,315	Henry	49,317	53,217
Coles	42,860	47,815	Iroquois	33,562	33,532
Cook	5,129,725	5,492,369	Jackson	42,152	55,008
Crawford	20,751	19,824	Jasper	11,346	10,741
Cumberland	9,936	9,772	Jefferson	32,135	31,446
De Kalb	51,714	71,654	Jersey	17,023	18,492
De Witt	17,253	16,975	Jo Daviess	21,821	21,766
Douglas	19,243	18,997	Johnson	6,928	7,550
Du Page	313,459	491,882	Kane	208,246	251,005
Edgar	22,550	21,591	Kankakee	92,063	97,250

County	1960	1970	County	1960	1970
Kendall	17,540	26,374	Pike	20,552	19,185
Knox	61,280	61,280	Pope	4,061	3,857
Lake	293,656	382,638	Pulaski	10,490	8,741
La Salle	110,800	111,409	Putnam	4,570	5,007
Lawrence	18,540	17,522	Randolph	29,988	31,379
Lee	38,749	37,947	Richland	16,299	16,829
Livingston	40,341	40,690	Rock Island	150,991	166,734
Logan	33,656	33,538	Saline	26,227	25,721
Macon	118,257	125,010	Sangamon	146,539	161,335
Macoupin	43,524	44,557	Schuyler	8,746	8,135
Madison	224,689	250,934	Scott	6,377	6,096
Marion	39,349	38,986	Shelby	23,404	22,589
Marshall	13,334	13,302	Stark	8,152	7,510
Mason	15,193	16,161	St. Clair	262,509	285,176
Massac	14,341	13,889	Stephenson	46,207	48,861
McDonough	28,928	36,653	Tazewell	99,789	118,649
McHenry	84,210	111,555	Union	17,645	16,071
McLean	83,877	104,389	Vermilion	96,176	97,047
Menard	9,248	9,685	Wabash	14,047	12,841
Mercer	17,149	17,294	Warren	21,587	21,595
Monroe	15,507	18,831	Washington	13,569	13,780
Montgomery	31,244	30,260	Wayne	19,008	17,004
Morgan	36,571	36,174	White	19,373	17,312
Moultrie	13,635	13,263	Whiteside	59,887	62,877
Ogle	38,106	42,867	Will	191,617	249,498
Peoria	189,044	195,318	Williamson	46,117	49,021
Perry	19,184	19,757	Winnebago	209,765	246,623
Piatt	14,960	15,509	Woodford	24,579	28,012

POPULATION AND PRINCIPAL CITIES

The 1970 United States census shows that Illinois ranks fifth in the nation with a population of 11,113,-976. This is a gain of 1,032,818 or 10.2 percent over the 1960 census of 10,081,158.

Most of this gain was in the cities. However, Chicago actually lost 183,447 people, as many middle class families moved to the suburbs.

Still, Chicago is by far the largest city in Illinois, with a population of 3,366,957—nearly a third of the people in the state. This makes Chicago the second largest city in the United States. (New York City is the largest.)

Where People Live

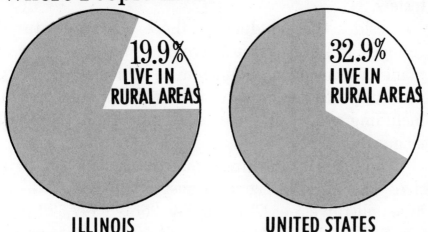

19.9% LIVE IN RURAL AREAS

32.9% LIVE IN RURAL AREAS

ILLINOIS   UNITED STATES

Population Per Square Mile

ILLINOIS   **UNITED STATES**

197.1 PERSONS PER SQ. MI.   **56.20 PERSONS PER SQ. MI.**

    Some 2,125,412 people live in Chicago's suburbs which fill the rest of Cook County. Many people commute to work in Chicago from cities and towns that lie beyond the suburbs and even from other communities beyond them. Altogether, the Chicago metropolitan area sprawls over eight counties in Illinois and Indiana and includes 7,612,314 people.

    Chicago became the nation's second largest city because it is a natural meeting place for all forms of transportation. A large variety of industries has gathered in and around Chicago to take advantage of this. The metropolitan area leads in the production of steel and food products. A number of industries, such as electronics, uses these products as raw materials.

Besides these industries there are ninety-three colleges and universities, five museums, two zoos, a planetarium and an aquarium in Chicago. The city also has professional teams in all the principal sports, including one team in each of the major baseball leagues.

No other city in Illinois comes close to Chicago in size. The state's second-largest city, Rockford, 85 miles northwest of Chicago, has "only" 147,370 people. Rockford is fairly typical of the downstate cities, as those outside the Chicago metropolitan area are called.

Rockford is the center of a large agricultural region and an important manufacturing city. Factories in Rockford make machinery, hardware, furniture and auto parts. The city also has an extensive park and recreation system and is the home of Rockford College.

Other Principal Illinois Cities and Their Populations

	1970	1960
Chicago	3,366,957	3,550,404
Rockford	147,370	133,522
Peoria	126,963	129,922
Springfield	91,753	90,401
Decatur	90,397	88,536
Joliet	80,378	73,480
Evanston	79,808	79,283
Aurora	74,182	66,253
Arlington Heights	69,204	52,900
East St. Louis	69,996	81,712

Skokie	68,911	70,178
Cicero	67,058	69,130
Waukegan	65,269	63,892
Oak Park	62,511	61,093
Oak Lawn	60,305	54,580
Des Plaines	57,239	50,789
Champaign	56,532	55,358
Elgin	55,691	49,447
Elmhurst	50,547	43,597
Rock Island	50,166	51,863
North Chicago	47,275	51,729
Moline	46,237	45,023
Quincy	45,288	47,583
Danville	42,570	42,457
Park Ridge	42,466	39,065
Chicago Heights	40,900	34,331
Granite City	40,440	40,073

THE GROWTH OF ILLINOIS

Year	Rank	Illinois	Chicago	Suburbs	Cook County	Down-state
1810		12,282				
1820	24th	55,211				
1830	20th	157,445				
1840	14th	476,183	4,470		10,201	
1850	11th	851,470	29,963	13,422	43,386	808,085
1860	4th	1,711,951	112,172	32,782	144,954	1,566,997
1870	4th	2,539,891	298,977	50,989	349,966	2,189,925
1880	4th	3,077,871	503,185	104,534	607,719	2,470,152
1890	3rd	3,826,352	1,099,850	92,072	1,191,922	2,634,430
1900	3rd	4,821,550	1,698,575	140,160	1,838,735	2,982,815
1910	3rd	5,638,591	2,185,283	219,950	2,405,233	3,233,358
1920	3rd	6,485,280	2,701,705	351,312	3,053,017	3,432,263
1930	3rd	7,630,654	3,376,438	605,685	3,982,125	3,648,531
1940	3rd	7,897,241	3,396,808	666,534	4,063,342	3,833,899
1950	4th	8,712,176	3,620,962	887,830	4,508,792	4,203,384
1960	4th	10,081,158	3,550,404	1,579,321	5,129,725	4,951,433
1970	5th	11,113,976	3,366,957	2,125,412	5,492,369	5,621,607

Source: "Illinois: A History of the Prairie State" (table inverted).

PART FOUR

GOVERNORS OF ILLINOIS

1818-1822—Shadrach Bond (D)
1822-1826—Edward Coles (D)
1826-1830—Ninian Edwards (D)
1830-1834—John Reynolds (D)
1834-1834—William L. D. Ewing (D)
1834-1838—Joseph Duncan (D)
1838-1842—Thomas Carlin (D)
1842-1846—Thomas Ford (D)
1846-1853—Augustus C. French (D)
1853-1857—Joel Matteson (D)
1857-1860—William H. Bissell (R)
1860-1861—John Wood (R)
1861-1865—Richard Yates (R)
1865-1869—Richard J. Ogelsby (R)
1869-1873—John M. Palmer (R)
1873-1873—Richard J. Ogelsby (R)
1873-1877—John L. Beveridge (R)
1877-1883—Shelby M. Cullom (R)
1883-1885—John M. Hamilton (R)
1885-1889—Richard J. Oglesby (R)
1889-1893—Joseph Fifer (R)
1893-1897—John Peter Altgeld (D)
1897-1901—John R. Tanner (R)
1901-1905—Richard Yates (R)
1905-1913—Charles S. Deneen (R)
1913-1917—Edward F. Dunne (D)
1917-1921—Frank O. Lowden (R)
1921-1929—Len Small (R)
1929-1933—Louis L. Emmerson (R)
1933-1940—Henry Horner (D)
1940-1941—John Stelle (D)
1941-1949—Dwight Green (R)
1949-1953—Adlai E. Stevenson (D)
1953-1961—William G. Stratton (R)
1961-1968—Otto Kerner (D)
1968-1969—Samuel H. Shapiro (D)
1969-1973—Richard B. Ogilvie (R)
1973-19 —Daniel Walker (D)
D = Democrat   R = Republican

PART FIVE

ILLINOIS TIME LINE

6000 B.C.—First evidence of Indians in Illinois.

A.D. 1000—Hopewell Indians.

1200-1700—Mississippi Indians.

1673—Marquette and Joliet are first Europeans to reach Illinois country.

1675—Marquette returns to teach Illini Indians.

1680—La Salle comes to Illinois country.

1690—Tonty receives trading rights in the area.

1696—Father Pierre Pinet's mission established at what is now Chicago.

1699—Cahokia founded, first permanent settlement in Illinois country.

1703—Jesuits establish Kaskaskia.

1717—Illinois country becomes part of French colony of Louisiana.

1720—First Fort de Chartres finished.

1756—Fort de Chartres rebuilt—most formidable on continent.

1763—Illinois country ceded to Britain by France.

1765—French flag lowered over Fort de Chartres.

1769—Chief Pontiac murdered by Illini.

1778—George Rogers Clark secures Illinois country for Virginia.

1779—Jean Baptiste Point du Sable establishes a trading post at Chicago; Illinois region becomes a county of Virginia.

1783—Treaty of peace with Britain recognized title of the United States to the Illinois country.

1784—Virginia gives up claim to Illinois.

1787—Northwest Ordinance establishes government for Illinois as part of Northwest Territory.

1800—Illinois becomes part of the Indiana Territory.

1803—Fort Dearborn established.

1809—Illinois Territory organized by Congress.

1812—People of Fort Dearborn massacred, fort destroyed by the Potawatomi Indians.

1813—Beginning of Peoria, Fort Clark built.

1814—First Illinois newspaper published.

1815—Beginning of Alton.

1816—Fort Armstrong begun, initiates Rock Island; new Fort Dearborn built.

1818—Illinois becomes 21st state on December 3; Albion founded.

1820—Capital moved from Kaskaskia to Vandalia.

1821—Springfield selected county seat of Sangamon County.

1822—Quincy and Urbana settled.

1825—First school law in Illinois.

1828—First steamboat reaches Peoria; McKendree College founded.

1829—Illinois College founded at Jacksonville; Decatur founded.

1830—Abraham Lincoln comes to Illinois.

1831—Joliet founded.

1832—Black Hawk War.

1833—Chicago chosen as terminal of Illinois and Michigan Canal; Chicago organized as a town.

1834—Aurora settled.

1835—Waukegan and Elgin settled.

1837—General Assembly passes bill making Springfield the state capital; Chicago incorporated as a city; Cairo settled; Knox College chartered; John Deere designs effective steel plow.

1838—First railroad operates in Illinois.

1839—Nauvoo founded; Rockford incorporated.

1843—Bloomington founded; Elmhurst settled.

1844—Joseph and Hyrum Smith murdered.

1846—Lincoln elected to Congress.

1847—First McCormick reaper plant built at Chicago.

1848—New state constitution forbids slavery, bans free Negroes from state; Illinois and Michigan Canal opens; Galena and Chicago Railroad begins.

1853—First state fair.

1854—Evanston founded.

1855—First comprehensive school law in Illinois passed; Kankakee begun; Northwestern University founded.

1856—Illinois Republican Party organized at Bloomington.

1858—Lincoln-Douglas debates; Lincoln loses election.

1860—Lincoln nominated, elected as president.

1861—Civil War begins; East St. Louis incorporated.

1864—President Lincoln reelected; Grant placed in command of Union armies.

1865—War ends; Lincoln buried; Chicago Union Stock Yards established.

1866—Cicero founded.

1867—University of Illinois founded.

1869—Grant becomes president.

1870—Third Illinois constitution adopted.

1871—Great Chicago fire.

1874—Segregation forbidden in public schools.

1875—Swift and Armour packing companies open in Chicago.

1876—State capitol begun.

1885—Jenney creates first skyscraper in Chicago.

1888—State capitol completed.

1889—Jane Addams opens Hull House.

1890—University of Chicago chartered.

1892—Granite City established.

1893—World's Columbian Exposition opens in Chicago.

1897—Chicago Loop created by new "L" lines.

1903—First effective child labor law passed in Illinois; Millikin University founded at Decatur.

1905—Hennepin Canal, also known as Illinois and Mississippi Canal, completed.

1913—Women's suffrage law passed by General Assembly.

1915—Steamer Eastland disaster, Chicago.

1917—U. S. enters WW I; 180,512 drafted.

1921—Cahokia Mounds studied for first time.

1931—First dramatic television program broadcast from Chicago.

1933—Century of Progress in Chicago.

1937—Oil discovered in Marion County, starting southern Illinois oil boom.

1941—World War II begins, 900,000 from Illinois serve, 27,000 killed.

1955—Land of Lincoln slogan adopted.

1959—Chicago becomes deep-water port.

1960—Dresden nuclear power plant begins operation.

1967—Weston chosen for nuclear accelerator; Picasso statue dedicated at Chicago.

1968—Illinois celebrates 150th anniversary of statehood.

1969—Old capitol opened after restoration completed.

1970—Illinois adopts new constitution.

Index